EVERYTHING I NEVER WANTED TO KNOW

21st CENTURY ESSAYS
David Lazar and Patrick Madden, Series Editors

EVERYTHING I NEVER WANTED TO KNOW

Christine Hume

MAD CREEK BOOKS, AN IMPRINT OF
THE OHIO STATE UNIVERSITY PRESS
COLUMBUS

Library of Congress Cataloging-in-Publication Data
Names: Hume, Christine, author.
Title: Everything I never wanted to know / Christine Hume.
Other titles: 21st century essays.
Description: Columbus : Mad Creek Books, an imprint of The Ohio
    State University Press, [2023] | Series: 21st century essays | Includes
    bibliographical references. | Summary: "Combines personal narrative and
    reportage to confront cultural and emotional reverberations of gender
    and sexual violence in America by examining assault cases in the author's
    hometown of Ypsilanti, Michigan, sex offender registries, and historical
    events such as the nylon riots of the 1940s"—Provided by publisher.
Identifiers: LCCN 2022041744 | ISBN 9780814258620 (paperback) | ISBN
    081425862X (paperback) | ISBN 9780814282694 (ebook) | ISBN
    0814282695 (ebook)
Subjects: LCSH: Sex crimes—Michigan—Ypsilanti. | Sex crimes—United
    States. | Women—Crimes against—Michigan—Ypsilanti. | Women—
    Crimes against—United States. | Sex offenders—Michigan—Ypsilanti. | Sex
    offenders—United States. | LCGFT: Essays.
Classification: LCC PS3608.U44 E94 2023 | DDC 814/.6—dc23/eng/20221005
LC record available at https://lccn.loc.gov/2022041744

Cover design by Susan Zucker
Text design by Juliet Williams
Type set in Sabon

∞ The paper used in this publication meets the minimum requirements of the
American National Standard for Information Sciences—Permanence of Paper
for Printed Library Materials. ANSI Z39.48-1992.

CONTENTS

ONE

CONSIDER

QUESTION LIKE A FACE

I am writing because they told me to never start a
sentence with because. But I wasn't trying to make
a sentence—I was trying to break free.

—Ocean Vuong

A decade ago, when I first arrived in Ypsilanti, I kept my eyes
open. The weekend we moved in, as we hauled boxes and decided
where to put the furniture, a stranger raped our neighbor in her
home. We tried to find a place for everything, including this news
and ourselves. We tried to find a horizon between settling and
unsettling, all the hinterland hours leaking shadow into sky. Our
neighbor had been raking leaves when she noticed a man watching her from across the street. The intensity of his stare hit her like
an emergency, and she ran inside. Suddenly right behind her, the
stranger yanked her arm hard. He raped her in the entryway, or
he tried to rape her and in doing so seriously injured her. There is
nothing to distinguish stranger and neighbor, except in our taking
a position. There is nothing to distinguish this event from count-
less others except that we were raising a baby girl and trying to
think of this neighborhood as home. We looked up and down our
street, hoping to exchange smiles with joggers, dog walkers, and
parents shuffling out the recycling, but our timing, our sudden
witness, seemed to embarrass them. Or maybe they were embarrassed for us, having chosen poorly, and heads down, they went
quickly back on their way.

3

As fewer people stopped to ask us how we liked the neighborhood, the days clarified themselves until stunned. Even the wide
streets, vacant buildings, and unkempt parks seemed constricted
by a glassy apprehension. As far as I remember, that winter turned
into a season of exceptional storms. This was voltage: a body
routed through its own pulsating vistas. I saw hours breaking
over an abundance of level land divided into two landscapes—one
always visible but never accessible and the other invisible even
though we crossed and recrossed it daily. We forget in both directions, but time had already taken shape in us as gender. We can
cut time and beat it, but it ultimately owns us. Every woman I
know here divides her life into before and after. Before the cancer, after the rape, before the child, after the assault, before the
divorce, after using, before leaving, before the election, before it
went viral, before the cops came, after time circles back for you.

Because two days after her death, a janitor found a student
in her dorm room, naked from the waist down, skirt pulled over
her head, with a pillow on her face. Suppressing this information,
the university reported her death as suspected suicide. Later, after
police located the man who raped then strangled her to death, the
university paid its president handsomely to leave town.

Because local law enforcement does nothing for a woman
whose ex-husband, after being locked up for aggravated stalking,
hires an inmate to kill her and their two sons. Because there is no
way to write an active sentence with her as the subject.

Because someone found a young woman dead in her bathtub, sexually assaulted and drowned. Her twin decides it couldn't
be the man who raised them, though all evidence points to their
stepfather. The case fades away as if time stopped at the moment
when no one could fathom it.

Because a woman runs out of her apartment, weeping, and
from my kitchen window, I see her looking over her shoulder
down our dusty alley.

Because a girl waiting at the bus stop outside the public library gets into her uncle's car and disappears for days.

Because at 4:00 a.m. her sister's boyfriend wakes her up to rape her in her own bed.

Because, as her former boyfriend beats her up, he damages the walls and floor enough to get her kicked out of public housing.

Because these are fragments of a communal story, we cook, work, mother, drive, and plan, but we sleep inside someone else's dream. We let our feelings dissipate across a screen. We listen to news without hearing the story, the accusations and backlash, the loopholes and dismissals we take for living. What makes us suddenly come into focus or get shoved into a shed out back has nothing to do with us. Do I even know one woman who hasn't been subjected to male violence? Do you? Why doesn't that admission stop us in our tracks?

What sustains me is knowing I can fabricate a story that allows me to sleep at night. Yet I'm humiliated by the bad faith that watches over my sleep. All women are from this invented place; we are from nowhere, which is the beginning of everything vulnerable and alive. We get ready, we prepare to be undone. Time slows, splits, and begins again after each lashing. Inside her house, a woman's habit becomes to wait for the next wave of rage. Time running as if there were a way out of staring at a woman's body, crumpled and unconscious on the living room floor. I imagine it frequently, with each *Post* or *Times* refresh. The dead woman can't look back, so I can stare at her for as long as I like. But I turn away, my body softens in a chair, and I think about tomorrow.

What is the thing in me that forgets? What allows me to keep walking past the house where a woman almost died; where she took it or fought back; where she cowered in a closet, begging, hands shaking too violently to use her phone; where she didn't see it coming; where she dragged herself, bleeding, to the front porch? What allows me to join the shrug of those who think there is nothing to be done? Nothing *I* could do? I feel time hurrying past me, washing over me, and with it comes the feeling that I would kill, too; I would beat and rape; I would kill in order to no longer despair. I would draw a house and lock you inside it. I would kick open the door. I would feel something heavy and sharp in my hands and instinctively raise it against you. What kind of justice forgets that we are all dangerous? If I weren't allowed to enter back into a life, I'd be a hundred men with a hundred ways of brutalizing; I'd be a hundred gun shots, a hundred thousand decibels coming after you. I'd be that because the civics of this place has turned us into parodies of ourselves: women curled inside light shards on the shadow-dappled wood floor; men fixed in the posture of forever looking into the blue distance, where after the hit, comes a bluer calm. Caught on the verge of our own aspirations, we get caught in the searchlight of a sentence. We are trying to get out of it alive.

In the mirror, I chase after my own innocence. I see a good coward, a nice victim. I see myself bruised and brutalized in the news, where women try to speak through convulsive crying, where we are shoved and shot and stolen away. Here comes the outrage of men who cannot protect their property, who cannot *do* anything. You might roll your eyes, I expect this. You might call the cops. A siren sound secretes into your laugh, and I feel my whole body set against it. I think, *today the only thing the women of Ypsilanti have in common is our refusal.* We say nope, I won't: react, show up, put that on, smile, encourage you, let you, comfort you. But resistance, too, is part of the script. I can't talk my way out of it or walk away from the street's metal and glass glaring at me. My eyes graze a gray utilities box where a man is tearing off a sticker; street artists call their stickers "slaps." This man peels off someone's slap in messy strips. He peels the slap of a Black woman's face. When I ask the man what he is doing, he says, "This is private property."

I catch her eye on the metal box. It's her only remaining feature, her watch. It's as if she staked her vision here. The rest is shredded in his fist. If she is private property or on private property, if she is flattened into an image of private property, where is the danger? There she goes, trashed all over again, ripped to pieces and shoved in his backpack. Then I see her whole face stuck on the window of a vacant building. I see her face on a city fence; her eyes fixed on traffic, her eyes fixed on me. Again on the back of a stop sign, and on blank spaces all over town, she returns like a refusal. Ask a boyfriend, and he will tell you she wouldn't listen. Ask a cop, and he will tell you she was resisting. Her face is a hole cut in time. When I look at it, her smile pulls me into a vast second, the careless moment of a joke, then I hear the gunshot. I hear her struggle louder than I hear mine. She repeats this moment all over town. As I'm waiting for the walk sign, the instant of her death returns, though I was never there. I was living my life, whose doors I lock. I will not die like that, not like she did. Hers will always be the face of a dead person to me—two-dimensional, black and white, pixilated—and each time I see it, I come closer to homicide. Minute by minute, we head into harassment, into assault, into murder. Into the incest-ridden desolation of child porn and rape. On every calendar day, her face repeating, the dead face replicating itself all over town, the story repeating, her story coming to find me like night finds day; it comes after you, her face like an outbreak of minutes, a pummeling. Because her face is where I can't find her, where I pass through each time I leave the house. I see it and am never quite sure I saw it. How many times, her face is telling me.

She had been fighting with her on-again-off-again boyfriend, who went outside to make the call. We hear yelling on the 911 recording, but we cannot make out the words or the problem exactly. When he sees the cops have arrived, her boyfriend walks back into the house, leaves the door open. Two cops follow from the dark yard with scorched pine needles sticking to their cuffs;

one of them had been here before on another domestic abuse call. In the police report, the cops kick in the door. They come into the hallway blinking and shouting. It's late. The couple is wrestling at the end of a dark hallway. The woman leaves the kitchen and walks toward the door with a knife in her hand. A tiny, curved fillet knife. Four-inch blade. Later the cops say she was "advancing," "coming at them" and "confronting them." A journalist describes her as "charging." The police report describes her as "wide-eyed" and "wild"; it says she "appeared to be in a deranged state," with a "blank stare." We know this part of the story, how language transforms her into a mad beast who cannot feel pain. Two cops bust into her house, shouting; when they are face to face with her, one cop grabs his Taser, the other his gun. This part of the story you've also heard: they both shoot and a real bullet shatters her heart. She falls to her left, faceup on the floor. All of this takes five to ten seconds: entering, yelling, killing.

A state memo says the "law of self-defense does not require that the least harmful means be employed before a more harmful level of force may be lawfully used." Cops can Taser anywhere on the body, but a bullet must go to the T-zone of the face or the center mass of the torso. A small woman who cooked to calm her nerves walks down a dark hall until her face is a door to memory; her face has no door. You get stuck inside it. Wait for what happens. Minutes replicate hours haunted by no specter of her suffering. What happens is night. What happens is the mayor calls her death "a tragedy of mental illness and drug abuse unabated." What happens is a story we fend off by dreaming up our own glorious escape. What happens is I'm compelled to respond to the mystery of this stranger, this dead woman, by reducing her to a calibrated mirror in which I both *see* myself and *separate* myself. I use a dead woman's suffering to sensitize me to my own pain. So that I can safely enter that pain and find my way out. I use her body, her face, to imagine my own suffering. I use this woman's face because race is the extent we will go to invent others in our service, but she does not belong to me. I know my whiteness will save me, will make me visible enough to become a headline and a hashtag, will make you feel accountable for me. I will get the full damsel treatment. You will be four times more likely to know about my abduction than a Black or Brown woman's. If a white woman goes missing, she will be described as attractive, slim, young, a mother or daughter. If a Black woman goes missing, we will be introduced to her mental health issues, her troubled past, her drug problem, her abusive boyfriend. That's the story we will hear. If she doesn't have a criminal record, her boyfriend or brother will definitely have one. And who do you think is more likely to vanish? Who is more likely to get hit? Who is more than twice as likely to be killed by an intimate partner? What *will be* slides decidedly into *what is*.

Even if you've never seen it, her face stands in for all the parts of writing that go away when I try to write about her. Her face echoes in the crude technology of memory that kinks like spent Taser wire. In the photograph you might mistake the scattered wire for scratches in the parquet under the kitchen table where chairs moved back and forth, recording each meal eaten there. When I was born, whatever happened in the home, stayed in the home. In the gap between then and now, our laws do a different kind of damage, while your own small voice keeps pleading. In that gap is where you get used to it. It is where a cop is more likely to lose his job for smoking a joint than beating his wife, and almost half of police families report domestic violence. A cop takes down her face here, but it reconstitutes over there. A citizen sprays black paint like a hood over her head, a blind spot where a face should be. Someone draws a penis with ballpoint on her forehead, but my daughter uses a handwipe to erase it. Because I am living in a city that proliferates a question like a face. Because her face appears and disappears on civic surfaces, because her face replaces a blank space; because her face replaces the city, piece by piece, claiming it, because her face is half hidden, in the half-light of waiting, half blowing in the wind, half stuck to the present, near a house where my family lives, where a young girl can look at it and think *not me*. Because a shunned person becomes a screen.

I **DO NOT** look at the Michigan Public Sex Offender Registry (PSOR) for the first ten years I live in Ypsilanti. I am skeptical enough of the legal system to know that the list isn't just about being an American man, but about being Black, Brown, or poor. It's about regulating sexuality. It's about moralism. It's about state control, surveillance, criminalization. It's about making people like me feel informed and warned. Are you aware that white men in early America executed hundreds of women for having sex with the Devil? The actual Devil. Our registry is also about Puritan shame.

But then I do one day, I look, and when I look at the Michigan PSOR, I stop breathing; I lose time because, despite all I know, I can count on my own repulsion. I'm caught in the horror of my own horror, which comes automatically and ambivalently. To find a way out, to find a way of thinking that feels less rigged and reactionary, I open other windows. I open up to history and context. When I dig under my horror, I find I am living in a city overwhelmed with debt due to toxic waste dumping; I find I am living in a city so poor that our skies take on airport traffic so that other cities don't have to; I am living in a city so poor that landlords welcome felons because the government pays the rent, a city of halfway houses and group homes. I find I am living in a city that claims one sex offender for every fifty-six residents. The ratio in the next town over is 1-to-1,312; in Detroit it's 1-to-214. In Ypsi, the number means one in twenty-six men living here are registered sex offenders. The number means within a mile radius of my house, ninety-eight sex offenders live clustered in sixty-seven clapboard houses mostly owned by someone else. Within five miles: 485. Tick, tick, the spectacle of faces, names, addresses on the registry blinds us to lives. These are not the men who raped, molested, filmed, sold, or held hostage anyone I know; perpetrators with resources tend to keep out of the law's reach. Because no one believes most women and children—the news feeds on delusional, mendacious, vengeful accusers. This is entertainment, and we love our outrage. Because most towns overflow with men who go under the radar, because most of this shit goes unreported— you know that. At the end of the day, it seems probable that most towns have undocumented numbers like the ones here. Don't even: no one here is on the list for peeing in public. Most are registered for rape or for involving someone under age thirteen in porn or prostitution or some other sexual abuse. These men may not be the men or not all the men, but the sheer normalcy of sexual violence arrives as a slap.

I walk with these facts backward into my own disappearance. The streets here are not endlessly alike, but they act like a maze when you are trying to face the other way. Circling back and seeing from different angles makes everyplace a trap. There is no direction I can go. I walk down Normal Street, where porches are memorials to women and children; they are buffer zones and luring grounds. On Congress, quiet becomes its own noise, a manmade silence forged from real silence. When walking with my daughter, she stops to marvel at the dead bird on the sidewalk outside a rapist's house. I look ahead for something to distract her, to move her along. But as crimes build up, these places go blank. The aftermath is forgetting. We're always claiming that everything in sight is a landmark of something beyond it. But do we know what our own bodies are leading us toward?

Walking streets all named after men—Washington, Sherman, Roosevelt—my attitude switchbacks in order to plot out emotional solvency. Because zigzagging is a good way to climb a mountain though there are no actual mountains here. From this angle: we are monsters; from the other side: they are monsters. Because offenders can refer to freedom only in the past, and women can refer to freedom only in the future. Because a woman can be blotted out or smeared into a rug's dystopian swirls. Just check the map, where the street view is obliterated by green dots indicating reports of sexual harassment and assault. Another map shows the homes of sex offenders, red upside-down tear drops flooding the topography. Each mark is a target. Each map reveals the bleak house of gender fictions, our doublethink, our beloved dualism. On one hand, *how much time is left?* On the other, *how long will we wait?* This way, that way. Put one map on top of the other and you begin to make out her face. Floating, saturated in fuchsia light. I do not understand, and I do not know how much I am trying not to understand.

The flatness of the land allows my thinking to go unbroken for hours, without resolution. Time holds what's not there until it is. I hold her face inside my dream until it comes alive. She runs and won't stop running all night because even in her dreams, they want to kill her or to sell her body. My grandfather, my friend, my boss, my boss's son, my teacher, my friend's brother, my boyfriend, a date, a dance partner, a guy I met at a party, a stranger on the subway, on the bus, in the street, a cousin, a cop, a president: they are after us in my dream. And we rush into their arms—because these are the traditions looking out for us. Their power wants us to feel watched over and protected; their power wants us to forget we gouged out our own eyes in order to live here with them; it wants us to look but not see what hides in these sentences and streets that end with her face. If you think her face riddling town signifies something different, you are fabricating distinctions in order to protect someone. Maybe yourself. We are all born into finite imaginations. We shoot a woman in her home or rape her there: either way it ends with her face plastered to the wall. It ends with her face.

CONSIDER THE SEX OFFENDER

The memory comes to me not as I'm driving my twelve-year-old to her first sleep-away camp in northern Michigan. It comes to me later that night as I'm falling asleep, in the dreamy limbo just before sleep, in the enchanted hour of exhaustion effortlessly turning to panic, that sweet spot reserved for self-sabotage. Drip by cortisol drip, I involuntarily recall a story I heard on NPR. A group of boys rape a twelve-year-old girl. In an abandoned hunting cabin in the woods. At a summer camp. In Michigan's Upper Peninsula. One boy lured her there, the others ambushed her. This is how I remember it. The violence marks the end of the girl's illusions of safety and strength. It marks the beginning of her false self, a personality presented as gift to the world, the one that can love and be loved when the real self is hiding in the back of a basement freezer. I remember she told no one. I remember her trauma not a moment before because I was waiting until there was nothing I could do to retract my daughter from the opening shot of that story.

Framing the NPR story with the mother's participation amplifies every wrong thing about it. And in retrospect, the scene where I left my only child—lakeside yurts, a treehouse library, zip lines and horseback riding trails—seemed a little too wholesome. My thinking while pulling into camp, *This is just like a movie set,* turns now to, *It was a front, a façade for believing in something that doesn't exist.* I *had been* alarmed by the number of grown men faintly furtive in the shadows, flashing too charming smiles, and the swarms of seventeen-year-old boys. When I express my concern to a friend, she exclaims, "sex camps for teenagers and the parents pay for it all!" What allows this to be funny is that she, unlike me, is imagining teenagers having consensual sex. We both know that by far most sexual violence happens between friends and family, not strangers.

But look around and the whole population feels like family. Michigan has the third largest number of registered sexual offenders in the country and the fourth largest per capita. Our small city, Ypsilanti, claims far more per capita sex offenders than the two "most dangerous" cities in America that also happen to be in Michigan, Saginaw and Detroit. Could I turn these fun facts into a different kind of story? *And off the girl goes, safely away from friends and family in our sleazy little hometown! Off into the wilds where all the forest animals gather around to protect her from her own kind.*

Here is something else I know: abuse begets abuse. It's one of the first things I learn about sexual abuse when I start reading about it in the mid-1980s. The books then called it a "cycle of abuse," with subheadings like "when victims become offenders." As a person who was sexually exploited as a child, I am haunted by the fear of repeating my history, reenacting it in a kind of zombie trance. Sexual assault leaves something below the skin: a magnetic impulse, a compulsion. It's as if sexual assault were a feeling or desire that wants to perpetuate itself, that needs a host to complete its life cycle. Picture this desire as a parasite. My perpetrator left a parasite in me. No matter how much therapy and yoga I do; no matter how many empathetic supporters I have; no matter how aware I become of others who share my experience; no matter how vigilant or well-intentioned I am; the parasite will control my behavior. Inevitably, I will act out the parasite's deep program. In this story, I am a host manipulating the scenes of my daughter's childhood into a familiar script, a horror show, a sad afterschool special. The opening shot of someone else's trauma memoir. Then we will both be zombies, and there's nothing a zombie likes better than company.

I offer an analog from the annals of nature: a parasitic fungus releases a mind-controlling chemical cocktail in the carpenter ant that eats it. The fungus hijacks the insect's central nervous system, which makes the ant march up the north side of a tree and bite down hard on a leaf. Once lock-jawed on a leaf, the fungus grows out of its brain for another ant to eat.

I imagine a parasite growing from my brain. Once I outgrow the target age, the nymphet stage, and have a child of my own, the parasite will force me to bait my own child. Perhaps even having a child, late in my childbearing years as my face and body became less girlish, was a desperate part of the parasite's project. Under its biological sway, I will do exactly what I need to do to feed my child to the pedophiles and molesters, the child rapists and pornographers. If I do not myself perpetrate those same horrors, I will find someone who will. My mother is a prime example of someone who used her daughter to reenact her own experiences of being molested. She could barely acknowledge her own abuse by her father, much less protect me from it. She left my bedroom door open, practically with an "enter here, pedophile" welcome mat. She left me for long stretches—days and months—in her parent's home, where my grandfather would put me on his lap as we watched cartoons in his bedroom, where he had easy access to my fold-out sofa bed in the early mornings. My mother may not have intended me to take her place as the child object, but she did nothing to prevent it.

My partner and I agree to talk with our daughter on the way to camp—not for the first time—about physical boundaries and what to do when they have been crossed. We are hours

into the long car trip to the other side of the state when everyone is still belting their favorite song, one after another, creating
a sonic shield. I decide that it's now or never and proceed; I ask
my daughter what she would do if someone touches her in a way
that makes her uncomfortable. She rolls her eyes, still singing, and
pantomimes her self-defense plan to the beat of the song: thumbs
in the eyeholes, knee to the groin. She makes a dance of it, singing and moving with the maniacal pulse of the pop song. Is feeling
strong and invincible the same thing as being it? I decide it will do
for now.

Nature is actually full of zombie creatures doing the dirty
work for their clever parasite hosts—a phenomenon known as
adaptive parasite manipulation. In Central America, ants that eat
bird droppings can end up ingesting a parasite that lays eggs in
their bellies, which transform the ants—turning them bright red
and round—to look like the local berries that birds eat. And one
domestic wasp, the emerald cockroach wasp, attacks with a neu-
rotransmitter-blocking venom that gives it control over the victim roach's body, which the wasp puppeteers into its nest, and
voila!—the living roach puppet has turned into larva food. Do
you think humans do not make slaves of one another? In North
Pole, Alaska, one in every thirty-five citizens is a registered sex
offender. Santa is the perfect parasitic pedophile and children
come pre-groomed to sit on his ample lap and keep secrets. We
must have a strict taboo and laws against sexually exploiting children precisely because we desire it.

I don't mean *you*, unless you do.

Sharing a bed with our children, as a necessity, convenience,
or philosophy, is an ancient practice that we work hard to protect. As attachment parenting becomes the norm—I count myself
among these ranks—we have unprecedented intimacy with our
children. The intensity of this closeness may directly correlate to
our fear of pedophilia, a fear that our intimacy might cross a line.
In the first year of my daughter's life, in a parenting book given to

us by one of our therapists, I read a throwaway line about the normalcy of feeling aroused by tending the baby. *Don't be alarmed,*
the book assured, *it doesn't mean you are a sexual deviant. The
feeling will pass.* Reading this, I wondered if intimacy and sexuality have become so divorced from one another that we might
mistake one for the other, especially when sleep deprived and in
the murky grounds of a new identity. The assertion of arousal as
a fact of parenting seemed scandalous to me at the time, but it
also gnawed at me until I became grateful—if a little daunted—
to know I could just acknowledge it as a fleeting phase. I never
did feel sexual attraction to my infant (perhaps I was doing it
wrong!), but I worry about people who do feel it, who get freaked
out by the feeling, identifying too strongly with it, fetishizing it or
burying it. In many cultures, pederastic relationships were considered part of the norm, with the relationship between the older
man and the adolescent boy ending once the boy was considered
grown. Other people's sexuality can be hard to fathom: weird,
creepy, confusing, embarrassing, recondite, or awkward. *I guess it
works for them.* When I look at some of my own past partners—
at humans I wanted—I cringe, unable to connect to the person I
was or find the thread of lust that led me to get with them. And
eroticism at its best is mildly panic-inducing and overwhelming;
no wonder it calls out extreme reactions. Put another way, who
hasn't had a sexual fuck-up or misstep or transgressive fantasy?
If my community ostracized me for each one, shame might super-
charge those moments, creating a personal erotic abyss, socially
impossible to climb out of.

GIVEN THE NEBULOUSNESS of sexuality itself, you may wonder
what exactly qualifies as a sex offence. Each state draws it differently, but here is the FBI's attempt to provide clarity: "Offenses
against chastity, common decency, morals and the like." Each
vagary raises the hairs on my neck a little higher. There are many

possible distinctions between kinds of sexual violence and their relationship to power, but the PSOR makes none. Michigan's three-tier system is a blunt attempt to acknowledge levels of severity. The easiest way to get a tier-three offense, which lands you on the list forever, is to commit a sexual offense against someone younger than thirteen, or to rape anyone at all. Of the hundreds of mostly men on the list in Ypsilanti, well over half have tier-three offences.

Recall that lone guy you sometimes see slinking around the children's section at the public library. He's not always the same person, but he's often there, too large and alone and using books as props. It's so common that dealing with this guy is part of the training manual—where a whole section is devoted to childless men loitering in the children's section—and part of the job in all three branches of the Ypsilanti Public Library.

Pedophilia is apparently irreversible; you just live with it. It controls your fantasies, your arousal, and your desire for a lifetime. Sounds a lot like plain old sexuality to me. Sounds a lot like a kind of mind-controlling parasite that makes us all act against our best judgement. In Edmund Spenser's *The Faerie Queene*, the character Acrasia is a witchy seductress of knights who possesses the Circe-like capacity to transform her lovers into monstrous animal shapes. I think of all the ex-lovers of mine and others that I've gleefully exchanged pillow talk about, the lovers we've all turned into the comedic, crazed, scary monsters and into slain and stalking animals. *Akrasia* is my mother's favorite word. It means the state of acting against your better judgment, or a lack of self-control, having a weak will. I didn't know it was my mother's favorite word until she ended her most recent email to me with the confession. Actually, I read it as an apology, or what suffices as an apology, I guess, for offering me up to the same man who sexually abused her. It's a code she knows I know. *Akrasia* is tied to sexuality by its use in the New Testament when Paul warns that a spouse withholding sex might encourage akrastic behavior. This is the exact excuse my mother offered me when I was in the eighth grade and finally told her about her father slipping into my bed the mornings we slept over at my grandparents' house. She asked no questions and only said, "I'm not surprised; your grandmother's a prude."

This is how statistics shake down into narrative. We like our transformation tales about women and girls to be brutal: we rape them and hold them hostage in our fantasies about rape. We indulge in the sanctimony of female vulnerability so that they can transform into "survivors" and "victims," but what then? Are we suspended in this defining agony forever? Unrelenting misery turns human beings into monsters. And poop becomes berries. A skull becomes a fungus pot. A molested girl becomes the mother of a molested girl. Because pain is a mother. A friend writes, "Have you heard about a man in a blue truck who has been reported trying to get girls into it? Sue told me that. We were just talking about how/when to let our girls go places alone. I guess never?"

Pedophiles by definition prefer prepubescent children, but only rarely are they exclusively attracted to children. Pedophiles are usually men and can be attracted to either or both sexes. In this way, pedophilia seems like a crime of opportunity. I doubt my grandfather, for instance, exclusively lusted for little girls, or that his compulsion toward children in his family was much more than availability and access. We like to think that pedophiles are made by other pedophiles—a parasite needs a new host—but chances are that being molested, raped, or sexually abused as a child will not make you a pedophile (but it might). Chances are you will simply arrange for your own children to become jailbait, as we used to say, but then again, you might not, or you might arrange it ineffectually.

These are not helpful thoughts when you realize you have left your tween girl to the wankers. I have sheltered her, to be sure. I have withheld information about sexual assault, not wanting her first understanding of sex to be colored by violence. I have fast-forwarded over rape scenes; I have not given her Snapchat or even a phone; I have limited her sugar and screen time. During her first week of public school, in sixth grade, she asked me to define *dabbing, twerking,* and *YouTubers.* I took her to the mall for the first time at age eleven. When we pushed through Macy's—like pushing past the coats to get to Narnia—she stopped at the threshold of the store, where it shoots you out into the mall interior. Staring dumbstruck with awe, she said, "there's more?" How was this girl going to defend herself against predator grooming? Against adaptive parasite manipulation? Against me, even, and everyone else trying to protect her?

Defendants in sex offender cases are treated as enemies rather than criminals. That we have enemies is undisputed. Maybe that is not the right word; *enemy* is a childish word, a word that simplifies and creates monsters. We have sides, we have opponents, we have greedy and selfish motherfuckers. But we aren't sure we can name them. We don't know who they are because we don't know who we are exactly. Are the pedophiles our enemies? Or the rapists? Or the citizens who want their names, addresses, and license plate numbers forever on a list?

MY FIRST SEMESTER of college, I wrote a satirical essay for class advocating for the castration of men before arrival on campus. This, I floated conciliatorily, might be a temporary measure to help women get through higher education without being raped or, I hoped, sexually harassed. In less than six months, I will have been both. I only remember the essay because of my teacher's adoring, exclamation-filled reaction to it and her suggestion that I read it aloud to class, which opened a window of nerve for me. In my speech class, I delivered a talk about sexual assault on campus that substituted the words *potential rapist* for the word *man,* which infuriated my entire class. If you think I was too much then or this essay is too intense right now, you are right. I did not transform the world with these stunts. Then, I became attracted to poetry because it allowed me to both tell and not tell, have a secret and confess at the same time. My mother's rebellion against her abuse may have been to keep secrets. By keeping something all to herself, by pretending she was what she wanted to be instead of what she was, she made boundaries where there were none. My style relied on shock and oversharing to steel myself against feeling vulnerable and preyed upon. I had plenty of great sexual experiences by then but no framework for understanding my relationship to sexuality. Later in college, I wrote an essay about having an abortion and about taking acid for the first time while pregnant, knowing that I would have an abortion. These academic acts felt provocative to me, and I courted a provocative edge. Had I grown up in the internet age, I shudder to think in what reckless and akrastic ways I would have used it. Luckily there were no ready cameras, no live tweeting, no instashame, no cyberbullying; people could move on, and I would move away. My daughter, however, doesn't have the luxury of being provocative or making sexual mistakes. Two days after she turned twelve, the US House of Representatives passed the Federal Adam Walsh Child Protection and Safety Reauthorization Act. This new law requires states to register children who have committed sexual offenses. Requires them. Children of any age. On the public list. Something you did in kindergarten could land you on the registry—and in some states—for life. Any teen can be on the list for consensual sex or sexting. A third party—say a parent—can make the claim. You might wonder who this law is protecting. Because something is against the law does not mean it necessarily causes harm. A ten-year-old acting out sexually probably needs therapy, not a lifetime of alienation and criminalization.

A century ago, masturbation, cunnilingus, fellatio, and sodomy were "unnatural acts" according to state law and medical texts. Broadly written anti-sodomy laws—which have been used to prosecute people as "sexual deviants"—only became obsolete in the twenty-first century. A dozen states still have them on the books even though the Supreme Court ruled them unconstitutional in 2003. In Michigan, it's still technically illegal to have anal or oral sex, but the antiquated law from 1931 is unenforceable at the federal level (and seventy-five years later it was revised to focus on animal abuse, while still actively addressing human sodomy). The legal definition of sodomy in Michigan is: "the abominable and detestable crime against nature either with mankind or with any animal." When a crime's definition *is* the crime, when we cannot even write it, we both deny and criminalize anal sex. The doublespeak runs back to a 1697 Massachusetts law that forbade "the detestable and abominable sin of buggery with mankind or beast, which is contrary to the very light of nature." At least in cases of bestiality, no one cares about the genders of the participants.

Around the corner from my house, two men on the list for child sexual assault and making child porn live at the exact address of the now closed Humpty Dumpty Day Care. How long have they lived there? When fewer children enrolled, the day care director overcharged their parents and started renting the top floors of the house to tenants. Eventually repeat violations including fraud and negligence shut down Humpty Dumpty. Down the street, a middle-aged man on the list for raping a minor now lives with his mom. Two blocks away, a man who had previously served time for trying to lure minors into a hotel room was arrested for filming boys in the locker room of the high school where he taught. Another man on that block tried to rape his granddaughter at her own high school graduation party.

This local list could keep going, and on a national scale, we see it daily in our headlines. Each story, once uncovered, feels like a revelation and a relief. Rather than face the relentlessness, we say, "there, he was caught," as if it were the end of the story. Once while travelling, I told my boyfriend I thought I had lice. We were on the train with plenty of time to kill, so he went looking through my hair. "There, I got it," he said, holding one up between his fingers for me, satisfied that the problem had been solved.

WHY, PEOPLE ASK me, do I want to spend my time thinking about sexual predation? I might say, "Male entitlement" or "twenty-five percent of the Supreme Court," or "the headlines every damn day," but I think, *It's the parasite.* Instead of leading my daughter into the sex offender's house around the block, with a cheery, "Be back soon!" I am thinking up arguments to get rid of the list altogether, to defend every human's right to be treated like a member of the community.

Parasites became a fascination of mine as a young adult, and I devoted hours to reading, writing, and talking about their amazing variety and resourcefulness. Then, it was clear who the enemy was and whose part I didn't want to play, what story I didn't want to own. This is where the metaphor exhausts itself. When I didn't realize what my fascination was tied to, I could have it freely; now I don't have time for indirection or stories I know too well. Getting older makes our own gross potentialities all too clear. What is it that you thought you'd never become? I remember the astonishment of many when I decided to have a baby. And who would have imagined that I could live in one place for two decades? That I would turn fifty? That I'd become a professor or agree to go camping? Or fall in love with someone without a taste for suicide? I'd like to think there was no way of seeing any of this coming. Who would have imagined this life? Now I know that I have less and less to scorn in others, that I have less and less to laugh at or pity in them, because there is nothing that I can be sure I could not become.

THE UNREGISTERED

Glances Toward and Away

Glance #1

If looks could kill, goes the expression, and in fact they can and do. To glance means to glide off a struck thing, to strike obliquely. We are talking about weapons now: to dart, to shoot—and about light, a blinding shine. Men have a way of glancing at women that lets us know we are already dead. They don't even need to be a good shot. Their flash shoots off. They look at you in the photograph or in the flesh. Makes no difference. It's a passing glance. But what is it passing for? The smug way that teacher looked at you in your high school library? We know early on that looking back is an invitation; they train us not to look back, to skim their faces softly, to sweep our eyes elsewhere, shift our vision to accommodate their gaze. You have seen this look your whole life, passing through generations of men. Your uncle eyes you as you stand up from the dinner table; his loaded glance over your body, showing you his "appreciation," then anger for your lack of gratitude. With the same look in his eye, your doctor, now that you are old enough to be alone with one, makes a pass at you. Do people still say that, or does *passing* mean you are only dying?

Glance #2

As I left my daughter in cabin "Carroll" at her summer camp for the arts, I wondered, "Did they name *all* the cabins after pedophilic artists?" I imagined the possible names of other cabins: girls sleeping in Polanski, Allen, Balthus, and Kelly; boys sleeping in Britten, Caravaggio, and Ginsberg. Perhaps my daughter's cabin isn't named for Lewis Carroll, but that's who comes to mind for me, a parent-writer leaving her daughter with strangers in the middle of nowhere. Carroll, the pen name of the man who wrote *Alice in Wonderland,* had a well-documented erotic fascination with children, photographing over thirty naked six- to twelve-year-olds. We do not have any evidence of Carroll's desires or even that his practice radically departed from standard Victorian sexualization of children, but his photographs do tell us something disturbing about his way of seeing children. It's this reputation that activates a primary parental fear. I don't joke to other parents or to my daughter about it, but my impulse to do so is distracting. I try to be silently thankful to this art camp for naming my fear, putting it right there on the door, as a kind of threshold that must be crossed, the gateway to citizenship within patriarchy. The sign says, *we aren't going to pretend that the Carrolls of the world don't pervade all places where children gather.* By refusing to look away from the sexual exploitation of children, I think, maybe I can stave off the danger. Keeping my fears in sight assures me that I won't be surprised when they materialize. I'll be ready. But then, naming the cabin "Carroll" might itself be considered a form of sexual harassment: a threat, a literal sign telling anyone who can read it that a girl's humanity matters less than her body, that girls are mysterious muses to old men until they are nothing. The forms of sexual harassment and misconduct morph as a girl moves through milestones, so that each stage of predation grooms us for and normalizes the next. A girl learns to be a vigilant object.

Glance #3

We talk about case studies instead of cultures. These cases become a ritualistic offering of hope and a false sense of justice. Yet famous bosses don't act very differently from yours or mine. For every limelighted husband, there's a thousand shadow-husbands. We know it's not the single incident that matters; it's not the glance, but death by a thousand glances, a thousand relentless stares and stalkings. Our fixation on targeting individuals is a copout when it comes at the expense of getting to the root of the problem: men at the center of everything. The National Sex Offender Registry (NSOR) only extends the logic of weeding out "the bad men." This list is symbolic because these are not—not by far—the only men. These are only the men who fit the (racist, classist, xenophobic, homophobic) description. These are the men who take a fall for the rest. When we out celebrity men, we use the words *fallen* or *taken down*, reinstating the hierarchies and power dynamics that created the conditions for their sexual predation in the first place. A few household names have been rebranded as everyday rapists, and it's not nothing, these outings, but it's a little like naming camp cabins after offenders or putting their names on a public registry. It's a mockery of the actual lives women and girls live. Every minute on earth, men sexually harass, badger, bully, abuse, and assault women without consequence. In my life, some moments of assault or harassment surprised me enough to remember, but most wove seamlessly into the fabric of the ordinary. I couldn't have articulated these moments as violations of my rights because I didn't think of them as anything particularly unusual. We all have our own personal lists, I guess, but I couldn't begin to name *all* the men. Not a single man who has harassed or assaulted me or anyone I know is on that official list. How many men is that? How many men *not* on the registry does it take to make that registry itself an offense? How many men are we talking? How many men are talking? We talk about the number of women who get raped every day, every year; we have those numbers, and we have the passive voice to help us avoid talking about the unregistered men who harass, abuse, assault, and rape.

Glance #4

A health care worker rapes a woman in a vegetative state, and no one knows about it until she has a baby. She had been in a vegetative state at a private nursing facility for fourteen years. What don't the headlines say? The word *rape*. They say the woman "had a baby," in total denial of the violatory crime that created the baby. We ignore and we pay attention to the wrong things; then we can't look away from the mess we created, which is too horrifying and implicating to sustain our attention. We find ourselves here—even after the case of Larry Nassar held us riveted. If we don't know what happens when parents are in the room, we are fully blind to what happens when they aren't. We settle into a comfortable neglect all over again, our sense of responsibility outsourced to cops and judges. The NSOR is our monument to disenchantment, marking our willingness to participate in systemic oppression as long as we feel "safe." Like Trump's Wall was, the NSOR is symbolic, which is to say an empty, evidence-less performance of protection. The most truthful yet useless argument against both is that they don't work. They are something concrete to point to and say: "we are doing all we can." Symbols tend to syphon off other kinds of protections as they fail to address the complexity of systems. *Safety* is a word that hangs with what we fear, with anything that needs regulation (says patriarchy, says capitalism, says religion) or can participate in the fantasy of control. The Oxford English Dictionary goes on for thirty pages about *safety* (noun), starting with "salvation of the soul" (French and Spanish) and "rights of sanctuary" (Latin), both a spiritual state and a deliverance. On one hand, children report pedophiles at least seven times on average before adults take them seriously; on the other, a lifetime of alienation and surveillance for those who do harm. On the one hand, most new sex crime is committed by first-time offenders; on the other, most men who have committed sex crimes are not on the list. On all the other hands, the threat of serving time or the criminalizing of men long after they have served time does little to help women and children avoid being the victims of sex crimes.

Glance #5

Each time I read about a celebrity outed for grossly wielding his power in exchange for sex, I involuntarily recall a corresponding memory. Something in the story always corresponds with my experience. Time opens a thought. Then another. The men I remember are unnamed, unlocated, unregistered. When I tell people about the stranger in London who used his hard dick to push me from the Tube platform onto a train—like a very short billy club—then stood on the other side of the closed doors and masturbated as he met my eyes through the window, I sometimes see disbelief on their faces, as if I were telling them my fantasy instead of my experience. I was eighteen years old, going from my job to my apartment, alone in a foreign country for the first time, on a crowded platform, with so many hips and elbows and bags jostling against me; I didn't know what it was until I turned around to face the closing doors. I saw him staring directly at me, and I saw everyone around me turn their heads away, as if ashamed for me, as if I had brought him with me, as if they were witnessing something private, as if they were all women who had to constantly negotiate and deflect harassment by looking away and getting on with their lives, pretending not to see it. I anticipate you looking away, too, as you read this; I anticipate your doubt because the averted looks of my fellow passengers taught me how to read the averted looks of my auditors when I tell the story: looking down or away, facing another way, about facing, leaving me alone with this stranger, coerced inside this story. Telling it years later to a table of writers got us kicked out of sports bar by an offended male waiter. He told us to leave, and we asked why. He said that our conversation was inappropriate and that other customers were complaining. What's worse than being harassed, I learned, is talking explicitly about being harassed.

The train lingered there for a long minute before speeding off. Cell phones did not exist in 1986, so I filmed it with my eyes, and I used language to make it into a story. I carry this experience around with me, to every place I go and live, until it becomes almost indistinguishable from all the others. It's a drop in the bucket: thousands of women have rhyming stories, local variations and regional varieties. I even have other stories like this one. Out of sheer exhaustion, we eventually learn to look away, to pretend we don't see, to screw our eyes into a distant star, to dig our focus into a stain at our feet.

Glance #6

Think of all the abuse Larry Nassar managed for decades while parents were in the room. Hundreds of girls and women, hundreds of parents, hundreds if not thousands of times. We turn away, or we turn a blind eye, an eye blinded by authority, groomed by authority blindness. It's the other side of gaslighting. If someone else can destroy my perception of reality by insisting on its inaccuracy, then I can preemptively disbelieve my own experiences and instincts. No parent could believe a doctor would casually

chat with them while finger banging their daughter. We put a lot
at stake in trusting the person wearing the white coat, in believing they will heal us, in not believing they have an erection while
inventing reasons to feel up minors. Culturally we see doctors as
sympathetic figures—who need therapy when they "fall"—instead
of as predators who must answer to the law. If the claims cannot be denied, these doctors get a diagnosis and treatment. They
come back, meaning most are eventually cleared for practice
again. When Nassar's case broke, it seemed like my small corner
of the world, Southeast Michigan, might be a hotbed of pedophilic pediatricians. Yet the scale of his abuse overwhelms and
eclipses regional news, thousands of house fires burning while a
forest fire rages. As the place fills with local smoke, we minimize
the damage. In 2011, a resident at University of Michigan Hospital, Stephen Jensen, received a minimum federal sentence for one
possession of child pornography. He was undergoing pediatric
training at the time. He left his flash drive in a hospital computer
where another resident found it and reported it to the attending physician, but Jensen wasn't arrested or reprimanded for six
months. In what sounds like a classic case of gaslighting, an attorney at the hospital told the resident who found the flash drive that
her concerns were "unfounded," never mind the ninety images
and four videos of child porn on that flash drive left in a public
computer in a hospital lounge. This man is so white, so middle
class, so professional, so doctorial, so male, that the final word
in the media about his case is this: "A tremendously bright future
has been lost," Jensen's attorney said. "He had a lot of potential to do a lot of good. He wanted to study cancer and cancer
treatments, and because of the way this thing went down, that
might be lost." The snuffed light of his noble future blinds us to
unnarrated pasts; clocks stay set around male empathy and identification. Time brands, burrows, blinks, double blinks. Memory
drops: male doctor, male doctor, male doctor.

Glance #7

My general practitioner calls in a nurse before starting my pelvic exam. She stands by the door, eyes fixed straight ahead—looking and not looking. My doctor asks me if there's anything I want to tell him before he begins. I am a little confused by this novel question. "No, I don't think so," I say, "like, what would I want to tell you?" My feet are already in stirrups. He peers at me over the sheet, "Like it doesn't bite or anything, does it?" As he chuckles and I do, too, in a startled and regressive attempt to make him feel less awkward, more comfortable, I catch the nurse giving him side-eye.

Glance #8

Winding down my two-year checkup, my otolaryngologist says, though my eardrum is "saggy," it appears to be doing the job. He says that I look young for my age. He says, it's okay to put my head under water. He says it's okay to stand on my head and to sneeze. As I'm gathering my things, he implores me to "avoid domestic abuse to the head." He says blows to the head would not be good for his work. "For my ear?" I ask. He says, "Yes, that might damage your ear and we'd have to redo the surgery."

Glance #9

A gynecologist tells me that I will have "the most watched breasts in Washtenaw County," a line he's clearly used on all the other 1,500 women whose boobs he "cares for." The line is extra creepy with its practiced, shticky half-laugh and his young female intern standing behind him as he sits way too close in a chair facing me. Embarrassed for him, my eyes instinctively dart to hers. I am in the *Handmaid's Tale* then, looking for surrogate comfort or recognition as the patriarch delivers his lines between us.

Glance #10

As I sit almost horizontal in the chair, my dentist keeps pulling down my skirt. His hand brushes my thighs over and over again as he literally yanks on my skirt right between my thighs. He does this as he looks in my mouth and again when he takes breaks from looking in my mouth. The most constant thing in the room is his hand yanking at the fabric over my thighs.

Glance #11

Looking requires an object; even projection needs an other. *How did I allow myself to become an object?* Women ask themselves variations of this question all their lives. Lacan tells us the gaze is separable from the eye. Once the ubiquitous male gaze has been internalized, we don't need an outside pair of eyes to trigger the feeling. We don't need men to perpetuate male supremacy. Women become actively exhibitionist, feeling ourselves cinematically as objects of desire, feeling ourselves through visual media, where the distinction between fantasy and reality blurs even harder. In becoming a spectacle, we find evidence of our own desirability, thereby becoming desirable in our own eyes. Recontextualized within a female body, the male gaze offers us this small consolation: by seeing ourselves the way we fantasize others see us, we outmaneuver the active/passive binary and become the symbol of our own desire. As a girl, this move stands in for real power; to an oppressed person it feels like power. The fifteen-year-old narrator of Marguerite Duras's autobiographical novel *The Lover* assumes her identity consciously and deliberately in relation to male desire in order to manipulate it, to subvert the equation by making passive active. This is all the freedom we are able to squeeze out of subjugation. All that passes for freedom in context. In Kristen Roupenian's 2017 viral story "Cat Person," it's how Margot thinks her way through unwanted sex; she imagines how turned on Robert is by her own "perfect body." She adopts his perspective in order to put herself at the center of her sexual fantasy. When men prove inept at sensual intimacy, women learn how to self-seduce.

Glance #12

In the dark, crowded theater, to get to my seat, I have to crawl over my daughter's first pediatrician, Howard Weinblatt, and his wife. I have popcorn in my hand as I step over his lap to get to the other side and settle in for *Blue Jasmine*. I had sworn off Woody Allen after he married his ex-wife's daughter, but we had a babysitter that night and we wanted to see a movie, so we settled on a sexual predator's film about sexual predation (via *A Streetcar Named Desire* and revenge at Mia Farrow). Years before this, and after we had already changed doctors, a local mother outed Howard Weinblatt's attraction to young girls. I was alarmed to see him, almost flaunting his status on the opening night of a Woody Allen film. He had been caught masturbating as he watched his tween neighbor, a patient since birth, undress on at least four occasions. The girl first noticed him watching her undress when she was ten. The mother filmed him watching her daughter undress and masturbating in his dining room window. No surprise that the police found exactly sixty-nine images of child pornography and child sexual exploitation on his computer, as well as a paid credit card subscription to the Pornhub channel Teen Dreams and a history of visiting various teen and incest-themed websites. Police used this evidence to pressure him into a no-contest plea to one count of sexual voyeurism. Another way of saying it is that he took a plea so that he would not have to answer to a child porn charge. Imagine this man: a short, white, sixty-five-year-old doctor, who practiced in the same community for over thirty years and volunteered in the local theater. If you Google him, you will find many images of him playing the life-eating maniac R. M. Renfield from *Dracula*. The character is a study in pathological addiction, where the compulsion to eat insects worsens and grows more deviant, culminating in the compulsion to drink a live person's blood. The metaphor is there for the taking. Many citizens rushed to imagine that Weinblatt himself must have been suffering from mental illness. That was the only explanation they could fathom. Is lust for children a mental illness? For fifty years it's been classified that way, yet our criminalization of it overshadows our willingness to treat and manage it.

Our country treats all sex offense as a criminalized addiction, impossible to kick. Once a personal erotic script gets written, it can exert an obsessive grip on the imagination. Though perhaps the even more pervasive mental illness is our collective impulse to protect abusive powerful men. In doing so, we protect ourselves from knowing what compulsive forces might exert themselves on a child's body, especially a body that an adult has access to under the guise of healing. We might call this willed ignorance by one of its names: *Nassar*. Did Weinblatt *nassar* his patients and their parents? Did anyone investigate his practice after his use of child porn came to light? How did his group practice handle his conviction? After his arrest, as parents of a former patient, we received a short-form letter from them saying he no longer worked there and expressing their contrition. Here's the thing: no one contacted us, or to my knowledge, any of the parents or patients about possible medical sexual misconduct. I read a couple of online comments, which don't indicate criminal behavior, but they merit examination if not alarm:

> Over the last year this man has given me his number to call
> him with concerns about my daughter's high risk health.

On numerous occasions he has told me to bring her to his house to give us a break. I keep replaying every office visit did i leave them alone? He kissed her and I thought nothing of it then. This makes me so sick to my stomach!!!!!!!!! How did he fool us all for so long? He was such an amazing dr- how could he have these demons??

My daughter is now 11 yrs old. Her pediatrician was in that IHA practice that Howard Weinblatt was in back in 2012. He wasn't her doctor, but I remember he treated her one of the times she had a bladder infection. I was sitting right there when he examined her. I don't remember anything inappropriate. I do remember when the examination was obviously over, I was the person who told her to pull up her underwear when that should have come from him.

You'd think a pediatrician with child pornography on his computer and a habit of masturbating to his tween patient while watching her undress in her own home might be someone you should investigate. I found out from the prosecutor's office that police did investigate possible sexual misconduct with three other children, but they did not authorize charges. Had Weinblatt not been an educated, white, upper middle-class, cis-gendered married man and a respected member of a powerful community, things might have gone a little differently.

Glance #13

Carceral logic forces its way into our imaginations at this point, extending the focus on bad actors instead of the structures that enable them. This sort of justice participates in the absolute devotion to knowing—to certitude and privilege—that allows us the satisfaction of turning our backs on selected perpetrators and does not even begin to address the problem. Our current laws around sex offense are false solutions, unevenly applied and rigged toward dehumanizing already marginalized men. It's a system of tokenization that works harder to cover up sex offense than to eliminate it. Don't forget that as a population, the enforcers of these laws—cops themselves—are four times more likely to commit sex crimes than civilians. Despite years and years of studies, we still have virtually no reliable evidence that sex offender laws work to reduce recidivism, and plenty of expert sentiment suggests that these laws may increase it. The NSOR fits easily into #MeToo narratives of accountability and the inadequacy of traditional safety mechanisms, yet it paradoxically undermines the larger goal of #MeToo to challenge the systems that perpetuate sexual harms. Once already-vulnerable populations become further criminalized and ostracized, they have very little to lose.

The NSOR merely stages a sense of security—an empty gesture of justice in the form of public disgrace and exile. As I write this, a sex offender compliance check sweeps through Ypsilanti but not its wealthy, white neighbor, Ann Arbor, where Weinblatt still resides, where Jensen was working at the time of his arrest, and where another pediatric doctor, Mark Hoeltzel, has recently been sentenced to ten years in federal prison for one count of online enticement of a minor. Since 2004, Hoeltzel has had a documented history of sexual relationships with minors and young patients, yet he only lost his medical license in 2017. Against all odds, these three local white doctors were caught, but all three had the luxury of plea bargains that allowed them to be sentenced for their least serious crime. Our legal system isn't built to hold middle-class white men accountable; they are honorary unregistered men, examples of who mostly escapes oversight, whose crimes and abuses get categorically overlooked and excused. If we cannot face the pervasiveness of sexual harassment and predation, if we pretend not to see what is right in front of us all the time— these are men you know and love as well as strangers and people

you work for and who work for you and who stand in line with
you at the grocery store and who live in your neighborhood and
your home—there is no way to correct our course.

Glance #14

In the aftermath of Larry Nassar, Michigan has pushed over thirty
bills through the House and Senate, ostensibly under the familiar rhetoric of safety. Some of the bills—expanding sexual education and requiring schools to keep records about why employees
leave—make sense in treating our national problem holistically.
Most of the bills, however, focus on punishment instead of pre-
vention. More laws leading to more imprisonment: stricter sentencing and higher mandatory minimum sentencing. Meanwhile,
we treat doctors like gods. Threat of punishment rarely deters a
compulsion in the overly privileged, the men who have been told
they are exceptions and exceptional all their livelong days.

Several months after they went into effect, these laws didn't
seem to touch Hoeltzel, whose six felony charges of receiving,
possessing, producing, and transferring child porn and obscene
materials to a minor were all dropped in a plea agreement.
Though pretrial sentencing called for almost double the amount,
he received ten years in December of 2018 for one felony count
of enticing a minor. Hoeltzel's first known target came to light
in 2006, when parents of an eleven-year-old patient discovered
two years of "inappropriate and flirtatious" messages from him,
many of which compliment her body and call her "sexy." In one
message he invites her out for ice cream. In response, his clinic
quietly asked him to take a "boundaries" course without further
investigation or reprimand. He returned to his practice weeks
later, and over the next eleven years, he left a long trail of sexual
harm and predation involving minors and patients, including creating a Facebook account for a fictitious boy, Ryan Gardner, to

chat online with multiple minor girls across the country and persuade them to produce pornography for him. He had hundreds of images of child porn on his computer and external drives. After his sentencing, the Department of Homeland Security's statement is revealing: "The sentencing handed down in this case reflects the serious nature of the crimes committed, which are particularly troubling given the defendant's role in the community as a physician. . . . This case shows that HSI [Homeland Security Investigations] is committed to investigating child predators regardless of the positions they hold in society."

This language begs the question. The bias is clear. In the imagination of Homeland Security, a doctor is first a powerful, respected community pillar, a status that overshadows his criminal activity. He is always first a doctor and not a child predator with special access to children. Does the perpetuation of obvious and ongoing discrepancies in the way we treat people who commit sex crimes matter as long as we admit those discrepancies? Does this HSI special agent think that offering a plea bargain dismissing the most serious charges, releasing him on bond (read: not seeing him as a threat), and under sentencing him for over a decade is evidence of fair distribution of the law and punishment? If anything, this case is a testament to the inefficacy of the NSOR and the ways professional white men evade the vigilant eyes of the law. The constant oversight of white men's wrongs creates a counter movement to make more laws, to get "tougher" on crime, and extend punishments, but it's not white men who ultimately pay the price; they aren't the men being over incarcerated and over surveilled.

Glance #15

I try to imagine a world where Weinblatt and Hoeltzel might be both held accountable and not shunned, locked away, or put on a registry. I try to imagine Hoeltzel getting the help he needed fourteen years before he landed in federal prison. I try to imagine a world that does not look away from the white doctor only to "overcorrect" the legal system in compensation. I try to imagine a world that does not repress white men's crimes while simultaneously projecting them onto and punishing Black and Brown men. I try to imagine a world where there aren't good guys and bad guys; there's just one fucked up America with the double curse of patriarchy and toxic masculinity, which has normalized predation on children and women for so long it's sometimes difficult to see. We turn away, we look blankly at the floor and wait for the gross guy on the subway to leave. I try to imagine my life without the exhaustion of managing male privilege and power. I try to imagine a world where the NSOR doesn't exist—it's underestimations not tolerated, its empty performance not desired, its vengeance not cultivated. I try to imagine a world where sexual misconduct doesn't disguise itself as routine exam. I try to imagine a world where a pediatrician doesn't use Facebook to convince fourteen-year-olds to send him homemade pornography. I try to imagine a world where "sexual misconduct" doesn't regularly masquerade as "dating" or a "business meeting"—where my hand isn't nervously on the doorknob, wondering if I'm going to be forced back in while my date/friend's father/boss isn't strategizing about trying one more time. I try to imagine what a woman who has not been habituated to these situations might do. Imagine a world where no cabins at summer camp, where no streets in town, where no civic buildings, where no schools, where no towns and no hospitals in those towns, are named after sexual predators. Imagine if sexual offense were treated as domestic terrorism, each incident another attack on our foundational institutions. Imagine if we faced our national problem together. We might rally behind children before they come to expect the worse from us. In this, ironically, we might take Weinblatt's own advice about talking to children after 9/11:

Dr. Howard Weinblatt, a pediatrician in Ann Arbor, Mich., said he told parents that rather than just blurting out everything they knew, they had to use their instincts about how much and what the child really wanted to know. And they must take their child seriously.

"That means stopping what you are doing," he said, and listening to what the child was saying. He has found that sometimes children, and even teenagers, have surprising misunderstandings.

On Tuesday evening, Dr. Weinblatt said, a 16-year-old girl was at his office for a routine visit. Suddenly, she started talking about the terrorist attacks. "She said, 'What's going to happen to the world now that they blew up the World Trade Center? Now there won't be any world trade,'" he said.

"Imagine how scary that was for that child," Dr. Weinblatt said. "But if you had not listened to her and just talked to her about how terrible it was, and that there was such a loss of life, you would have missed it."

Weinblatt knows about looking and he knows about turning away. What he says here offers an uncanny understanding about sexual abuse and harassment, one that doesn't distract us or overwhelm us with the sexual. After all, sex might be a stand-in for power—manipulation, deceit, and the psychic violence of being fucked with—in the dynamics of abuse. If we just "talk about how terrible it is," if we assume our positions as violator and victim, if we cling to blindly inherited logics of gender, if we focus intently on this or that one case, we miss the big picture, the large-scale connections and systemic enforcements; we miss the chance to see through our own glancing, to see through our assumptions and insurances. We miss the chance to embrace looking as a vehicle to understanding, its precarity and terrors intact. We miss the chance to free ourselves from the tyranny of turning away and its overcompensating consequences, the scramble to legislate, to register, to react in the name of "safety."

OUR FAVORITE COSTUME IS THE ONE WE FORCE OTHERS TO WEAR

Do you believe in the Boogeyman? The question sounds like a taunt or a dare, which is exactly its function in the movie franchise *Halloween.* Whoever believes has half a chance at surviving. Yet to recognize and name the boogeyman is another problem altogether: "it" or "him," "thing" or "human," "The Shape" or "Michael Myers?" No matter what the movie's doctors, cops, journalists, children, babysitters, and grandmothers call the boogeyman, we understand him as a man going after girls and women. We understand him as a man-shaped monster, a monster hiding inside a man, using a blanched, balding Captain Kirk mask to show both his monstrosity and his humanity, his irresolvable condition strobing.

Even if you have never seen the original movie, you know the plot. On Halloween night, 1963, six-year-old Michael Myers kills his older sister after she has sex with her boyfriend. We see the scene through the boy's perspective; the camera wears his clown mask creating for us the effect of looking through a peep hole or binoculars. The boy climbs the stairs, knife in hand, then sees his naked sister brushing her hair and humming in postcoital dreaminess as she looks into a mirror. We hear Michael's heavy breathing and his sister's screams that sound more like she's having sex than being stabbed to death. As viewers, we participate voyeuristically in the hypersexualized killing. The final shot of his sister spread suggestively on the floor—her breasts staring up wide-eyed, her eyes closed—recalls the actress's past as *Playboy*'s Playmate of the Month just a few years before.

Cut to 1978, when Myers, after being locked in an asylum for fifteen years, escapes back into the neighborhood to reenact his crime on teenagers, who, like his sister, use the freedom of baby-sitting to have sex with their boyfriends. His brutality answers the open sexuality of these young women; to enjoy themselves as sexual beings costs them their lives. Yet Myers is perversely figured as a fantasy boyfriend—half creepy stalker, half shy loner. Only the bookish and virginal heroine, Laurie Strode (Jamie Lee Curtis), defies Myers by fending him off with a knitting needle and a coat hanger, domestic objects that reinforce her image as the "good babysitter" and "virtuous girl." We understand the story as a morality tale embedded within a coming-of-age story.

Halloween ignited the 1980s craze for slasher movies, a genre targeting sexually active teenagers. These films clearly tapped into a zeitgeist frantic with anxieties about sexual predators lurking in American high schools, summer camps, rural towns, and suburban subdivisions, anywhere teens might congregate without supervision. Living inconspicuously among us, the predator in these films, *Halloween* included, is the boy next door gone inexplicably wrong. Myer's diagnosis? His doctor calls him "purely, simply evil." He is a kind of phantom: a half-imaginary eruption of our nightmares, an embodiment of sexual sublimation and our libidinal investment in violence. We've internalized him without believing in him. He is the boogeyman, a force older than the genetic code. What we know about him is that he has always haunted our imaginations.

Halloween is the perfect mise-en-scène for our struggle to define our identity, our humanity, by feeling around its edges. Fear of adults wanting to harm children on Halloween has been with us at least since the 1960s, when media reported a rash of booby-trapped apples, a premise right out of a fairy tale. Whose Halloween in the 70s and 80s was not given a booster of spookiness with tales of poisoned—LSD-enhanced, cyanide-laced—treats? We had thought razorblade-spiked candy was a prank, a bit of folklore to shore up the occult mood, until our parents took our candy to the local ER to be x-rayed or made us break every piece in half before we ate even one. Over fifty years of candy vigilance hasn't turned up even a single case of tampering or contamination of Halloween stash from strangers.

Cut to the fall of 2016, the height of the evil clown sightings and reported attacks on children. It seemed everyone that fall had a creepy clown story to tell or video to show, set somewhere nearby, somewhere clowns should definitely not be: schools, woods, and parking lots. According to these stories, clowns were hurting or abducting children. Walmart and Target pulled clown masks from their websites. Police across the nation started arresting anyone dressed in a clown costume. Clowns are scary because they are meant to captivate children with their transgressive antics and dramatic foolery. Stephen King's *It* is based on the serial killer John Wayne Gacey, who taught himself how to apply clown make up and made his own clown costumes, which he wore to gain proximity to children. Michael Myers's first mask is a clown mask. These men were not kidding. In Michigan during the evil clown hysteria, many parents called off trick or treating, or they armed themselves for it, some shooting a few warning rounds into the woods just in case. But, of course, the scare began as a marketing stunt for a horror movie. The real horror unspools once people become terrified. We court fear when the promise of rescue is nearby. We wear the costumes of clowns, witches, and monsters that we love to imagine or fear becoming. We say "trick or treat" as if telling the truth about power.

One person can infect a town. Ancient Thebes is cursed by the "unnatural" act of Oedipus killing his father and marrying his mother, and the whole town suffers. Haddonfield, Illinois, a Midwestern suburb, is cursed by Michael Myers killing his sister.

An alienated loner now living within the community that formerly rejected him comes with baggage. His house is dark, filled with as much emptiness as we can bear, and we rush toward it, heart pounding. Haddonfield could be a portmanteau of Holden Caulfield, the protagonist of *The Catcher in the Rye,* who tells his story to a therapist in a mental hospital. His famous red hunting cap as well as his fixation on children, his self-pitying anger, his ambiguous allusions to past sexual aggression, and his trouble connecting to girls his own age resonates with the classic profile of a pervy predator. A boogeyman for every town, or in our case, thousands of them.

We might know the Boogeyman—he's our neighbor, our doctor, our teacher, our coach. In this incarnation of him, he is indistinguishable from a dad; he might even be our dad, as he was for Laura Palmer on *Twin Peaks,* David Lynch's 1990 television show that turned on these fears. His danger lies in his familiarity; maybe we've said hi to him in the parking lot; we could have easily encountered him mowing his lawn or playing with the neighbor's dog. He's polite and charming—think Larry Nassar and Humbert Humbert. In a variation of this incarnation, he is rich and powerful and looking at you—think Jeffrey Epstein and R. Kelly and Donald Trump. Men are scary to teenage girls because they are first their fathers—protectors and providers—and then their lovers; teenage girls live in a world where they have both fathers and lovers. Sometimes the two get confused the way violence and love sometimes do.

In another incarnation, the boogeyman appears in the archive of Halloween, a statistically improbable true stranger, the one who lurks waiting for you to separate from your friends. This is the boogeyman we most fear. The children's section of the library, the bus stop, the playground, the shortcut through a corn field on the way home from school turn out to be exactly the same place, and in all of them he is called "monster." Anyone can wear a mask; in this way, anyone can be made into a stranger. Michael

Myers is both the boy next door and a stranger; he reaches deep into both incarnations of the boogeyman, compounding our alarm. He is voiceless and mostly faceless, a vacancy onto which we project our fears.

Let's begin again with another child's disappearance. A child ghost for every day and the everyday stranger who raped and killed them. Named Jessica, Megan, Polly, Amber, Chelsea, Adam, Jacob: white, middle-class victims are everywhere in the media. A spate of laws passed since the mid-1990s were named after these children, whose whiteness makes their tragedies national spectacles. Each new law—Adam Walsh Child Protection and Safety Act, Jessica's Law, Megan's Law, Jacob Wetterling Crimes Against Children and Sexually Violent Offender Registry Act, Chelsea's Law, Amber Alert—aims at protecting children from "stranger danger," a largely mythical threat. Strangers commit only three percent of sexual abuse and six percent of child murders.

The *Halloween* franchise, with its monster who escaped from the asylum, coincided with the onset of our national stranger danger campaign and the tail end of the deinstitutionalization movement that a decade prior had freed juvenile offenders and mentally ill patients, placing them in community-based care facilities. As public policy, deinstitutionalization began with John F. Kennedy's Community Mental Health Centers Act of 1963, which aimed at combating abuse, neglect, and misdiagnoses in asylums and was sustained by the invention of psychotropic drugs. The massive influx of former asylum patients into established communities, however, without proper infrastructure or public education, stirred up distress and stigmatization. Psychopaths were coming to the neighborhood! Monsters were coming to steal our children's innocence! As a commentary on the deinstitutionalization movement of the seventies, *Halloween* proposes that mental illness is akin to criminality, which when read through stranger danger propaganda of the era, means sexual predation.

This fear remains with us today. It has been codified in draconian and unconstitutional laws aimed at sex offenders, who we imagine are men like Michael Myers, capable of shaking off morality and bullets to keep destroying lives. Since 1994, when it was launched, the NSOR has been legally othering sex offenders and making it almost impossible for them to feel like a normal part of the community after they have done their time. Laws dictating where former offenders can live and work ensure that they remain strangers. Once we make them put on their sex offender costume, we make sure they never take it off. On Halloween, so-called "no candy" laws address our fears about these imagined malevolent strangers. Throughout the US, Halloween night triggers myriad state, county, and municipality procedures for sex offenders, some of which have been on the books since the 1990s. The real setting of the fictional *Halloween*, Illinois, was the first to codify Halloween restrictions in 2005. California, Delaware, Florida, Georgia, Louisiana, Missouri, New York, Nevada, North Carolina, Ohio, Tennessee, Texas, Wisconsin, and Wyoming have since followed. Laws and statutes sometimes target all registered sex offenders and sometimes only paroled sex offenders. Every October, local police and the media act together to issue safety tips that point parents to the PSOR and stage "random" compliance sweeps, guaranteed positive coverage in the press. Under California's "Operation Boo" and New York's "Halloween: Zero Tolerance," police and parole officer sweeps enforce strict state-wide curfews and round up homeless or transient sex offenders for the night. If a registrant forgets to update a phone number with their parole officer, a Halloween-night home visit might lead to a felony charge. In my own county, cops enforce social death by rounding up every person on probation for a sex offense and holding them in the education room next to the jail for the duration of trick or treating. What if we were all locked into perpetual punishment for our future potential crimes? The future is replaced by punishment for a coming crime.

No matter what offense they've committed, no matter if they lack a sexual or violent history with children, no matter how ineffective it is in stopping future offenses, "no candy" laws mean that sex offenders must post a sign in their yards: "No candy at this residence." Or they must tack state-generated "No candy, no treats" signs to their front doors. They cannot drive after dark; they cannot decorate their homes, inside or out, for Halloween; they cannot have parties in their homes that night; they cannot answer their door between 5:00 and 10:00 p.m.; they cannot have their porch lights on or their window treatments open. They cannot hand out candy. They cannot go on hayrides or go into haunted houses or corn mazes. They cannot dress as a cop. They cannot wear a doctor or clergy costume. They cannot dress as Santa. They cannot dress as Captain Kirk. They cannot dress as Michael Myers. They cannot dress as a clown or a monster. They cannot wear any mask or costume because we know the sex offender is already wearing one.

Yet sex crimes do not spike on Halloween; no more or less of it happens on the night we ask to be scared. To boot, almost all the sex crimes committed by strangers on Halloween are committed by first-time offenders. Registered sexual offenders aren't often repeat offenders; the only offense with a lower recidivism rate is murder. Children are by far more likely to get hit by a car on Halloween than become a victim of a sex crime. The dangers on Halloween are far more familiar and domestic than we like to believe. Take the case of five-year-old Kevin Totson, who supposedly died from heroin-spiked candy but was actually poisoned by his uncle's supply in 1970. Or take the case several years later of eight-year-old Timothy O'Bryan, whose cyanide-laced pixie stick came from his father who had just taken out a life insurance policy on the child. There is simply no proof of any child in the United States being injured or killed by tampering with Halloween candy.

Who is the monster now?

Who is the boogeyman who cannot recognize a human being when we see one? The scariest thing might in fact be the horror that happens in the service of our own safety. It might be what we see looking back at us in the mirror.

PEOPLE HATE FACTS. When confronted with them, we stick to our impressions. Our feelings persevere even in the face of contradictory data. We trust our gut. We tell our children to trust their gut feelings, to know if an adult's touch is "bad touch." But our guts are promiscuous and pre-groomed, teeming with culture: we are not even certain what's in them. Our family's guts are full of the formidable bacteria and germs from all the places we've lived: strangers and shit and the tender ghosts of children. Bacteria cannot break down feeling into facts. Our gut feelings cannot make culture perceptible beyond information about it.

A few years ago, in our own neighborhood we noticed a patrol car sitting in the dark, under an elm tree across the street. The cop inside beckoned trick-or-treaters to his window and gave them candy. Perhaps in a clumsy attempt to obscure that police might groom children to take candy from strangers, the patrol car now cruises the neighborhood on Halloween, lights flashing, decorated with cobwebs and a skeleton riding shotgun. "Ghostbusters" loops loudly through the PA system. Though a cop, or at least someone dressed like a cop, still hands out candy from his car window, the roving spectacle is another part of the theater of safety for the middle class. We think we can tell Halloween's heroes from the villains, but just watch.

We don't so much overstate our fears as misdirect them. We fear the wrong things then make laws that theatricalize safety while actually amplifying our vulnerability. These laws fictionalize danger then stage protection. We think we can make laws anywhere we feel threatened, we can draw the line, we can tighten the porousness of borders on Halloween no matter the harm in that impulse. The way things are, we think, is not our fault. But when pedophile predators are props for Halloween, so are the laws that disappear them. We walk straight into the setup, desperately wanting to disrupt our own tidy fantasies, our false narratives about sexuality and power, danger and safety. The story itself is a force inside a holiday, inside a law, inside a neighborhood.

Who are the "no candy" laws protecting? What are they preventing? They prevent parents and everyone from the truth about the security of children. By validating public panic instead of educating us about bona fide dangers, they prevent us from making laws that actually protect us from sexual violence. They prevent former offenders from rebuilding their lives and safely rejoining their communities. They are emblematic of a whole arsenal of restrictions and notification laws that evidence suggests do more harm than good, actually increasing the likelihood of re-offense by imposing economic, social, and psychological burdens on released offenders. Our practice of scapegoating only the registered prevents us from our own vulnerability, our immersion in everyday patriarchal entitlement and American masculinity. It protects the sex offenders who we invite into our lives, who we live and work with, who we love. It prevents us from reexamining the fright and dread that shaped us as kids. It prevents lawmakers from looking closely at the failure of the legal system to handle any form of sexual assault.

Do you know what I mean when I say to banish a person from humanity, from community and care, is to ensure their monstrosity and ours?

The NSOR is an industry worth billions of dollars. It turns people into commodities. It turns calendar time into commercial time. It turns doing time into a life sentence. It turns a holiday into a horror movie, and it turns horror movies and ghost stories into laws we believe in. We live in a haunted house but see boogeymen out in the shadows and on the registry. We can browse our neighborhoods on the PSOR like a menu of avatars or genres of boogeymen. Some of these people have done appalling things, to be sure, but what happens when we never allow them to change costumes? We treat registrants as if they share a common psychological profile, something akin to "purely, simply evil," but what many of them do have in common is economic, political, and social marginalization. That is, they are not in power. But what about the children, we say; can we at least save the children? Even after all this, that's what we say when we mean to save ourselves the trouble of saving anyone.

GHOST WALK

(Tour of Ypsilanti)

This guided walk is intent on summoning ghosts: the ghosts of who we were and who we thought we would be when we imagined ghosts guiding us into a better time. We're retracing the steps of our last big protest to mark what didn't take hold. By walking forward through our small city, we're moving back in an attempt to bring time itself up to speed. We all have in us phantom sounds of these marvelous women and fallen machines, our collective outcries. We begin on Main Street, at the crossroads. After the sex offender's inauguration into the highest public office, this is where we held cardboard signs and flooded the streets, ready to catch fire, to make everything burn. We were frothy-mouthed, chanting and shouting, syllables spiking around us like swallows caught in an updraft. Our voices—perched, aloft, twisted, floating, diving—filled the sky. Some of our voices shook like branches. Some were panoramic. Some were like tongues sliding back down our throats. All together, we swarmed and flexed. We called names. It was unusually warm that January day. My friend stuffed our jackets into her bag. A gang of fathers with babies whose mothers had joined the larger march at the Capitol also carried open-mouthed bags gagged with sweaters. We filled our lungs and mouths with hot sounds, invisible and vibratory and pissed. But our throng of marchers couldn't keep their chants from falling apart, syllables chasing a syntax that turned on itself: see how easily "Love trumps Hate" becomes "Love Trump's Hate?" We caught nothing on fire. We had forgotten that to be a woman walking in the streets would return us to catcalls, threats, accusations, assaults, even when we are the ones shouting. You can hear anything you want in that roar, you can even hear fire, even the flames of hell, and even a paradise that arises out of hell. "What's a pretty girl like you doing out here?" one of the cops says, smiling.

Déjà Vu Showgirls, 31 North Washington Street

As we passed the local strip club, one neighbor heard his own name in the chanting, and once he heard "I hate Mark Maynard," he could not stop hearing it. In other words, the ghost words that snuck out of our chanting seemed personal. They came in waves we could ride out, subliminal or formerly repressed sounds about men. Something my neighbor was incapable of saying even to himself was making itself heard at the rally. Not a true voice but an internalized one bubbling up from a memory or a movie, one of many possible voices scattered and buzzing through the city. The man he was afraid he might be was coming into earshot. Did we hate him? He did not ask. What had he done to be hated? We answered silently. Who knows what any of us might start hearing, what death might acquire a voice inside us. Think of songs that come back to you involuntarily: the military band at your father's funeral, your seventh-grade choir's set ("Like a Rhinestone Cowboy," "Somewhere Over the Rainbow"), the first song you knew all the words to on the radio ("That's the Way (I like It)"), drunken revolutionary songs you learned abroad. The song playing ("Quinn the Eskimo")—but from where?—while you were being raped, while he held you, humming and half singing. Words pulsed and strained to make themselves intelligible. You might throw your voice up into the chant and it might take shape there;

you might feel an anger coming up through your feet, edging itself into your consciousness. The chanters were all of these sounds, a gathering signal that hollowed your marrow. Listen to them. Who hates you? I'll tell you: the people of the future hate you.

Ladies Literary Club, 218 North Washington Street

Right here, in the 1870s, a small group of white women decided to study together. They wanted to "keep up" with their men, and they read books, silently in solitude, all the while having passionate conversations in their heads that always outpaced the real talk they managed when gathered together. How to retrieve those spontaneous thoughts and words that were so vivid while reading? The women purchased this clubhouse in 1914, a coup at the time, and their discussions grew more authentic. Between the strip club and this library club, Ypsilanti packs the entire range of sonic representation of white women in America. Police whistles, pregnant silences, parroted sentences, ingratiating murmurs, shrill objections, long overdue 911 calls targeting the wrong person at the wrong time. We were suddenly sick of ourselves, our very own sounds, and shouting down the streets. Women are always ready to believe in our own improvement; ready to make ourselves over, to pull ourselves together, to work harder, to be better, to sacrifice more, to endure, to forgive anyone but ourselves, but to let ourselves off the hook anyway. We wear our softness around us like a fog that might smother everyone in town.

Rapid Shoe Fix, 115 Pearl Street

It's difficult to see what went wrong. In our fog, we took at least one wrong turn, then blamed our shoes. It's a lot to ask of a shoe, to carry you to freedom, to register at four miles per hour what has happened in a time warp, to walk ourselves into a place and time, to inscribe and to resist inscribing ourselves in this story. I have resoled or re-heeled at least a handful of boots here at Rapid Shoe Fix, some multiple times. My shoes don't ruin me, but the world makes shitty shoes, and that world does ruin me; it continues to manufacture delicate replicas of frail shoes that create the circumstances of my fall. If I am taking tiny steps or limping, if I can't keep myself on the sidewalk, I blame my shoes. This tour is no Take Back the Night march, but when I hear a woman running, her snow boots crunching the snow, her breath heavy, I feel the heat of her shame. I remember a girl in flipflops splashing a puddle on the sidewalk, where a shady neighbor placed a hose as a lure on a hot day. We know this hose is a jerry-rigged solution to his flooding basement, but we also know full well about weather, opportunism, and desperation. He watches the girl from his window. He thinks about his wet basement and the erupting wells, pirate streams, lost rivers, buried canals, the watery caves lapping with fish, the slippery ground the city is built on. We live in a place where water shapes topography from below ground. Put an ear to the earth if you don't believe me.

Riverside Park

The Huron River, to your right, once powered the Ypsilanti Underwear Company's mill. Women workers huddled every morning to chant slogans like, "If love runs cold, do not despair, there's Ypsilanti underwear." Let's try chanting together; the melancholy and whimsy of these chants could not be timelier: "A sculptor of bacchantes / Omitted the panties / So a kind hearted madam who had 'em / Supplied them with warm Ypsilantis." What does it mean for a place to rhyme with *panty*? Can we ever escape it? Below the water wheel, someone painted an enormous woman dressed in a tight-fitting union suit. What you saw on even the shittiest days

was a lady-monster towering ten feet over you. Even from the passing train, she seemed to loom, omniscient and demanding. Your
breath sucked out of you as she suddenly filled your train window.
Tiny buttons running down her torso. What you heard was deafen-
ing, the sound of a damned river pouring through, pounding down
into itself. Ypsi-made underwear was exhibited at the 1893 World's
Fair in Chicago and prized by the Prince of Wales. Imagine that
tall drink of water dressed from ankles to collar bone in Ypsiwear.
This was the underwear of progressive folk; it was the underwear
of the health reformers, recommended by the medical industry.
Made with merino wool and silk thread that the company promised would not ride up your ass or roll up your leg while you rode
a bike to work. I wonder who managed the backflap without frustration first thing in the morning. I think about trying to get the
seed buttons undone to pee in the middle of the night. The buttons
seem ill-suited for adult hands, but they also might give a potential rapist enough trouble to make escape possible. Perhaps getting
access won't seem worth the bother; perhaps he will give up on
such a sustained project. Or find a different hole. Perhaps I will
have thought to hide a weapon in their wealth of fabric. But what
if the rapist had small, deft hands or was a child or simply busted
the buttons off with one terrible yank? After the underwear company collapsed in 1906, a knitting company took over, then the
Brotherhood Maintenance Corporation, but nothing stuck. Neglect
turned the building into a fire trap. A ghost building. The Huron
rushes by the ruin and through the heart of town. But the women
workers, those phantoms wandering in our path, we step aside for
them as they come toward us, we step aside so they don't have to.

Thelma Goodman's Fashion Center, 415 Harriet Street

We didn't march by this address, but we should have. So much
of the history of women here has to do with what didn't hap-

pen, with negation or refusal. Doing one thing means not doing another. Thelma Goodman did not have her husband's permission, but she went ahead and gave herself the time and space. She wanted to imagine a life for herself outside the factory. During Jim Crow segregation, Goodman created a store and beauty salon that allowed Black women to shop and try clothes on freely. Because this place did not exist at the time. First the shop was in her basement, where women talked and laughed and sotto voced "what do you think?" Because we did not march here, we did not see that Thelma's store no longer exists. We did not see the office building now for sale at this very busy intersection, on the corner of two one-way streets, Huron and Harriet. Our chants were direct, one way, and we had escape on our minds. We had only the freedom to say "that's mine" on our minds. Harriet Street is named for Harriet Tubman, one of the only streets in town named after a woman. Most streets named after men use their last name or name the thing they have killed. Harriet Street was the heart of the Black business district until the construction of a nearby highway—then city dump—made it impossible. We foreclosed on the future of women many times. When medical schools in the middle of the 1800s told recent immigrant Helen McAndrews "no," she just kept at it until she found one willing to take a chance on a woman. This was her whiteness working. When she got back to Ypsilanti as a certified doctor, no one with any status acknowledged her expertise. But she showed them. She built a Bathhouse, a water cure, with vapor, mineral, and sitz baths, and she urged those idiots to scrub their minds clean of ignorance and meanness. People came from all over to take her cure.

Parish Inn Bed and Breakfast, 105 South Huron Street

This house we are walking past now was hers, Helen McAndrew's. Susan B. Anthony stayed here, and so did Mary Livermore, another suffragist and abolitionist, who, on this spot, delivered her famous public health lecture "What Shall We Do with Our Daughters?" In it, she took the fashion industry to task. A father I know recently asked his daughter if she could kick off a rapey date and run away in "those shoes." When he asked this, he was unknowingly echoing Livermore's lecture. And his daughter told him so. "I've heard that before," she said. How close does Livermore come to victim blaming? Bullseye. But she urged women to walk and be vocal as well; she wanted women to feel their bodies as agents of transport and discovery. She wanted us to run fast. If you think fashion is frivolous, put on a corset from that era and try moving, try shouting and not passing out. Try to escape your cage. We cram ourselves in the tiniest moments. We squeeze into outfits. Fashion shows us what we think of women. It's fitting that this site is now a Victorian-style bed and breakfast in ornamentation overload: high, flouncy beds with delicate flower prints and tall, hand-carved posts; lace pillows stacked in tidy rows. You will find overdressed furniture and plenty of mirrors in which to cry. You can sob silently, shaking, wet-faced, with an open mouth, voice jammed into your heart, or you can howl. There are a million ways to cry out loud—whimper, weep, wail, bawl, yowl, blubber, convulse, keen, snivel. Waterworks, they call it when you turn it on. Not because anything works, but because you need to dissolve. And sometimes you need to watch yourself dissolve in the mirror to make contact with your own feelings, to finally make some noise about what happened. You find self-empathy by watching yourself cry. "Go ahead," you say to your reflection, "go ahead and tell me." What surfaces when you do finally say aloud what has happened to you? The voice—your voice—sounds unrecognizable, and what you say doesn't sound real or true. Each time you say it—and you must say it repeatedly to remind yourself or to believe yourself—it sounds more rehearsed and more untrue. You forget a detail here, you misremember the sequence of events or the exact words. How could you say it so calmly, so deadpan, so everyday? Is there a way to make your voice sound real when you say what happened? Look into the window's reflection now and ask: How do we make ourselves exist? How do we make ourselves as real as this window, this brick wall, this fence, this proliferating garden?

Community Garden, corner of Normal and Congress

There are marigolds here now, but most of the year, just snow. Marigolds keep mosquitos away, they fend off unwanted things. Witches used marigolds as charms against the plague and gossip. I love their difficult smell and that they are easy to grow, which makes the marigolds that don't come up in Toni Morrison's *The Bluest Eye* mean something: "We thought, at the time, that it was because Pecola was having her father's baby that the marigolds did not grow." Mary's gold is where it gets its name. Mary's honey pot, her weeping pussy, makes Mary every kind of woman, including me. Yesterday at the public library a man called me an "easy pussy," then after he went back to browsing the library's new acquisitions, he returned to tell me that "an easy pussy is exactly what it sounds like." Victorian flower language links marigolds to cruelty toward loved ones, but this man was no one I even know. The ghost of a word crosses my mind: pussy willow and weeping willow portmanteau into a joke. When I leave the library, it's pouring. As I'm running to my car, I hear the man in the library's voice, "boo hoo, boo fucking hoo!" Maybe I'm hallucinating? Did I look confused? Did I look sad or hurt? Did I look "easy?" No one seems to be around when I get to my car. I spot a patch of dried-up marigolds getting soaked in the rain, and I remember living abroad as a girl, feeling very American at my fifth birthday party as I gave each my friends one marigold planted in a Dixie cup as a party favor. I find myself fantasizing about being abroad, about another country, another world, another dimension, better than here. Then my mind returns as if to say let's not forget geological time: marigold time, dirt time, insect time, rock time; let's not forget historic time—when we were property, when we were nothing irreplaceable.

Recreation Park

I'm taking us on a course correction here. This park is where dozens of women have been sexually terrorized since my arrival in town, and it is also where decades of rallies for women's suffrage took place. It's large enough to accommodate both and a little windier than everywhere around it. This park might be where you hold your breath, trying to move through it without being noticed except by off-leash dogs. You can see this park now looks ordinary—joggers, community gardeners, swingers, kite flyers, basketball players—but this is where the vote was finally won in 1918. I like to imagine the suffragists—with dirty dress hems sweeping the grass and snow and mud—shouted together, feeding on one another's clarity. After the first attempt at women's suffrage failed, the movement organized more seriously, and they felt their brawn right on this spot of land. Plus, it's in the neighborhood where the most famous Rosie the Riveter (Rose Will Monroe) used to live, in a boarding house with her two kids. I recently saw two grown women dressed as Rosie the Riveters in front of me in line at Value World. Because they were near the Halloween rack, it took a second to register that they were in costume. They told me they had just broken the Guinness World Record for the number of Rosies gathered in one place: 3,700. "We took the record back from California," they said. "And it belongs *here*," I responded, getting into the spirit. Here is where Ford's Willow Run bomber plant once claimed more than 20,000 Rosies. It was the first manufacturing site to employ women on the assembly line. These women could produce a B-24-E Bomber—a.k.a. the Liberator—in fifty-nine minutes, the fastest of any plant in the nation. By the end of the war, the Willow Run Plant had produced over 8,500 of them. These two Rosies were celebrating with a birthday month coupon at Value World. After they left, though, I realized how quickly I got caught up in their "you can do it" solidarity. I admit, Rosie the Riveter has always left me a little cold and confused. This is feminism? Smells more like military propaganda and capitalist iconography. And it turns out our local wartime Rosies were white supremacists. Our white Rosies aggressively fought for years to keep Black women out of the plant. Ford claimed he couldn't hire Black women because the white Rosies vehemently opposed it, but in truth, he didn't want to hire *any* Black workers. And Ford walked away from the plant entirely in 1945 when Black United Auto Worker members won seats on City Council in an attempt to force the issue. The same can be said for many suffragists—they were fighting only for white women in the name of all women.

Candy Cane Park

It's a short jaunt to another park, memorable for its mildly creepy name, a little too close to *do-you-want-some-Candy* Park. It should be named after the twelve-year-old who challenged the American Little League's boys-only policy in pre–title IX era. As with women's suffrage in Michigan, this girl, Carolyn King, initially lost, but being at bat had taught her what a second chance means. In 1974, she won, and then the Little League was forced to allow girls to join the team, to compete, to play. I'd like to think she haunts the park, this pre-teen girl who is now about the age where it would not be a tragedy to die. I'd like to think she shed something of her youth here in the hard shadows that never accumulated into a statue of her. She was a girl with an arm. She was a girl who could run. She was a girl who wanted to play. Now when we see a baseball diamond, we don't think of Carolyn King, we think of pitchers and catchers, of stealing and striking out. Baseball is great as a game, though its structure has been widely adopted as a substitute for thinking. Take our use of it to talk about sexuality as something that's competitive and staged, something that has landmarks one must move through—first base, second base, third base—until someone becomes won over, slain, defeated, victimized, and someone else scores. All that talk about bases replicates itself in the risk assessment scale—or in Michigan, the tier system, based on crime and not risk—which is the set of criteria used to classify criminal sexual misconduct. The more violent the assailant and the younger the victim, the higher the tier or risk. On the surface that seems reasonable, but most sex offense isn't violent because the victim has been groomed. In both disciplinary frameworks (the scale and the tier system), if no force or threats are involved, the crime in the eyes of the law is not as serious. Over 45,000 people have been "tiered" under the Sex Offender Registration Act in Michigan. While the pandemic was in high gear, in December of 2020, parts of the Michigan SOR Act were ruled unconstitutional. In response, the tier status of people convicted of sex offense will no longer be made public and the school zone exclusion will be lifted so that registrants can live near or visit schools. None of those schools feature a statue of Carolyn King, a schoolgirl knocking it out of the park, a girl who asserted her equal rights, who claimed her bodily rights without it leading to a full loss of credibility, who won in a court and a game, neither designed for her.

The Hiker, intersection of Washtenaw and Cross

Instead, there is this Spanish War Memorial and across the street, a bust of the failed Greek general who lent Ypsilanti his name.

Both are on many-tiered pedestals. How many women did these two men beat, harass, and terrorize? What town doesn't have a statue of a man with a gun? Here is ours, one of them, a gallant man with a hat and a gun, The Hiker, which is what an American in the Spanish Civil War called himself. His boyish charm makes it easy to believe that he was happy to go to war, that war is like a vacation from life. Where can women go to take a vacation from this bullshit? At the unveiling ceremony in May of 1940, a congressman used the occasion of a war memorial to advocate for peace: "Murder is murder wherever it is, whether in Japan or France." The statue says to me now, patriarchy is patriarchy wherever it is. Boys will be boys; a hiker will be a man walking since the war began. Whatever the latest war is, he walks so that we remember it. There are more than fifty identical Hikers across America, armed and walking into battle from all directions. He is here to remind us: we are already in the fray. We walk inside a war and there's nowhere it does not exist, nowhere to walk away from or into. Every circle you walk draws a ring around one territory of the war. Can statues serve as warnings? Can they be haunted by twelve-year-old girls? Can they face the future instead of the past—even if we have to crane our heads skyward to see the heroic figures, standing contrapposto, silhouetted in the sunlight?

The Water Tower, 303 North Summit Street

Take a deep breath. We are here, where we've always been headed. Our city is marked by one defining structure, and there is no escaping it. Our entire city spirals out from this water tower, our key landmark, the monument that underscores all monuments, and featured on the Top Ten Phallic Buildings in America list. Yes, there is a list, look it up. The water tower seems to come straight out of the ground, fully tumescent, loaded with bricks, crowned with a head. If our town is known for anything, it is known for this "brick dick," as we affectionately call it. Though it is unmarked as such, we use it to commemorate our local sex offenders as well as attract others. This dick-shaped tower in the center of our town was around for a hundred years before the registry, which is its symbolic double. You could fit all the names on Michigan's PSOR inside the tower and we'd still drink from it. It's eerie, how we feel, standing beside it, the full heaviness and the toweringness of systems made to fuck us over. Arising from a little spit of land flanked by one-way streets, the sex offender monument is on the highest ground in the city. You see it coming and going. On one side is the University; on the other is a row of houses in which about twenty registered male offenders live. The plaque here gives an account—a Queen Anne style limestone tower with crosses embedded in interior walls and so on with the nitty gritty of mechanics and function. It's easy to read right through crosses being embedded in our infrastructure because the official language masks the tower's cultural utility as a kind of flag for sex offenders. I had for so long wondered why sex offenders picked Ypsilanti to live—was it the cheap housing? the lack of schools and parks that for so long they could not live near? the other offenders? Maybe this monument calls to them, a visible symbol of welcoming and weeping. Old-timers say that any local terror caused by sexual harm gets plunged into its steel interior and held there until the voices suffocate, change color, until the reverb shreds vowels, protecting us from the trouble of being censored by the state. Another rumor or joke about this tower is that it will crumble if ever a virgin graduates from the University. Shall I pause here for your laughter? The city stopped offering tours of it after 9/11 because you can see the entire city from the top. The whole city visible on a clear day, and from up there you can sweep your shadow-arm over the city; you can hold it all in your palm.

Bell Tower, Halle Library

Those are the University library tower bells you hear. Our library bells evoke many pasts when their ringing was thought to protect plants, guide the lost, clear the air, break lightning, and repel ghosts. Their pulsations set the world right. One book in this library describes how bell vibrations were once thought to act as a mystic inseminator. In this way, the library tower seems in league with the water tower, forcibly transmitting both history and modernity. The bells are meant to assure you that time keeps going, the march of time keeps you humming and haunting and counting minutes until the next sex crimes on campus. The bells clang out musical standards as if played by car horns, if the horns were actually bells and if rapes could be stopped by bells or songs or chants or screams, traveling two miles on a misty day.

Tap Room, 201 West Michigan Avenue

Here we are, last stop, at one of the historic bars in town. Notice the door to this bar. The handle is not quite three feet off the ground. This handle was carefully placed to accommodate the little people who Ford employed last century in the cramped center assembly wing of the Willow Run bomber plant. They hired only people with dwarfism for this wing of the plant. Capitalism finds utility and fetish in our bodies. The city built itself with certain men in mind, but there are plain monuments like this door to show that others lived here, too. This door—we should paint it gold and leave it open!—makes you want to walk through it, dragging your tired ideas like a train wreck behind you. A body is not a door. You want to walk through it now, walk into a popular burlesque drag show every Tuesday. You walk through the memory of a crowd of men, chanting and shouting along with you until their phones distracted them or you did, until they curb-crawled you, until they commented on your hair. They say, "come on, have a little fun," then "don't be such a bitch." You walk through time.

You've walked with me into the way a city feels inside a woman, inside our day and night, uncertain and erased, all surface and slipping, inside seasons and the earth's rotation and ovulation or not, bleeding or not.

TWO

YES, BUT

FROZEN AND PHANTOM WINGS

The Body in Pieces

As a Gemini, my astrological profile tells me that my best physical feature is my shoulders, blades and all. This feels like a joke or a euphemism, how you'd compliment an ugly woman. After my divorce, when a boyfriend told me I had beautiful feet, I thought, *so it's come to this.* Shoulders may be more obviously sexy and less fetishized than feet, as the trend for off-the-shoulder asymmetrical and cold-shoulder tops demonstrates. If you don't know a "cold shoulder" shirt or sweater, you've definitely seen them: the shoulders are literally cut out, neat round holes like anti-bras, to display two curves of flesh, which become, in situ, proxies for boobs. We become four-titted. The god with a hundred eyes, the goddess with a thousand arms, the human with four tits, merging the two real ones with the two shoulder-tits in the mind's eye like 3D projection. Some say the butt is also a surrogate for boobs, your back boobs. Because the owner of the back boobs can't easily see you looking, you can look for as long as you like; you can see the displaced boobs without the complications of a face and identity or even being seen yourself. The butt is the voyeur's boobs. We call breasts "our girls," suggesting they are both metaphor and metonym; we are both part of their "girlhood," and they stand for our whole self. We Arcimboldize our bodies with specialized sexual characteristics. We have boobs coming and going, but the mystery of shoulders, like that of butts, should remain opaque.

A body repeats itself; it reproduces freely the parts we must publicly leave to the imagination. My college boyfriend showed me how to move, either by folding or cutting, the knees of the Native American woman pictured on the Land-O-Lakes butter carton up to her chest, transforming knees into breasts. From 1928 until the company removed the woman from their logo in 2020, consumers passed along this "trick," amplifying the sexualization and exoticism of the Land-O-Lakes' racist icon. Subliminal messaging in advertising at the time still felt newly conspiratorial. To my boyfriend, the trick took pleasure in calling out the company while at the same time participating in their racism and sexism. My boyfriend couldn't believe I had never seen this before, and I would have been happy never to know it.

Knees, shoulders, butt cheeks—anything can become boobs. This might be lucky considering how many women lose their breasts to cancer. My mother had a mastectomy at age thirty-five, a fact she kept from me until I was almost twenty, long after I puzzled over the prosthetic in her underwear drawer. She is not someone who willingly gives up her secrets, but I had been persistent in my curiosity and suspicion. When she told me, I felt in her long, shame-fueled silence a familiar *how could I not have known?*

Is this feeling more common to woman, especially middle-aged women? We are often surprised by our own bodies. *How come no one told me? Why have I never heard of this before?* We neglect to mention how we've been medicalized, how we've scored a new diagnosis, how a decade itself becomes diagnosable as if any age past forty were itself a disease that suddenly inducts us into a yet another club that we didn't know existed. Seeing ourselves through the male gaze—where we are all surface and appearance, cut off from our own blood and guts—is often our first de facto perspective, and as if to return the favor, our silence about our bodies protects the male gaze. Even my dreams bifurcate my vision: I am audience to my own imagined horizons, which I experience in both first and third person—at once the aerial view of flying and the grounded view of seeing myself in the sky, flying off, the shadow of my own body passing over me.

Maybe I haven't been listening, or I've been listening through my own biological and trauma-triggered pride. I grew up athletic, confident in my body, but also believing that I was in control of my own objecthood. Polycystic ovaries, menorrhagia, or thyroid problems were something, like cramps, that happened to the unlucky. You can't tell by looking at my shoulders that one of them is clinically "frozen," meaning that for the past year, it won't move.

Do I have a chip on my shoulder?

Do you want to cry on it?

SHOULDER, AS BOTH a noun and a verb, suggests difficulty. When you feel the weight of the world lift, you feel it first in your shoulders. In the novel I'm reading, men are characterized by the "continual use of the shoulders in carrying a spade, planks, sacks of potatoes, and tired children on the way home from the fair." You can shoulder in, shoulder a burden, or put your shoulder to the wheel, and always the point is effort.

Cold shoulder is a survival skill within a patriarchy. It means to silently turn your back on someone in a willful performance of defensive ignoring and disdain. When we give men the cold shoulder, we are trying to short circuit an entire system of harassment and objectification, trying to opt out of privileging male attention over our own desires. When Anna Burn's narrator in *Milkman* says, "his predatory nature pushed me into frozenness every time," we recognize the feeling. Every time.

Though inaccurate, the popular folk etymology of *cold shoulder* has something in common with the feminist cold shoulder.

In medieval England, the story goes, a guest who had overstayed their welcome might be served a cold cut of mutton shoulder, the toughest part of the animal. In doing so, the host communicated without words that it was time for the guest to hightail it out of there ASAP. Our meat does the talking until we become the meat. We eventually construct a false etymology out of the simple fact that a cold cut of mutton was a poor person's meal. The actual first reference to the phrase in print is Sir Walter Scott's *The Antiquary*, 1816, which features a mistranslation of the phrase "stubbornly they turned their backs on you" from the Vulgate bible. Because the Latin *umerus* means both "shoulder" and "back," Scott's error turned into a new idiom: "The Countess's dislike didna gang farther at first than just showing o' the cauld shouther."

Everywhere men are serious, women are cold. When I was diagnosed with "frozen shoulder," I laughed. *Is that a real condition?* It was both obvious and obscure. Had my cultivation of a cold shoulder, my capacity to ice out men's advances, made my shoulder actually freeze up, something like the parental threat *what if your face freezes that way?* In middle age, my cold shoulder had become an atavistic trait, an obsolete gesture, an overdeveloped skill that, apparently, atrophied into a state of pure "frozenness." My shoulder became a headstone's curve of immoveable granite memorializing my previous life as a sexual being in a sexist culture. I no longer needed it.

I resisted this reflexive metaphoric thinking as soon as it wasn't my own voice delivering it. When echoed back to me by experts I had sought out for help, pathologizing a biological condition, making vague references to repressed feelings, it sounded offensive. *Was my frozen shoulder the result of unexpressed anger and frustration? Was it a punishment I'd guiltily wished upon myself?* Of course, I know that our internal lives are inextricable from our bodily ones; I know, too, how neurosis has been and continues to be leveled at women in particular. So much of what happens to women's bodies remains baffling and embarrassing to the medical establishment. It's well known now that female pain is categorically underestimated by doctors, and in clinical trials and research, the male body is taken to be the standard, the default, the ideal against which all other bodies become measured. They have no idea why frozen shoulder happens or how to stop it. It has something to do with menopause or thyroid dysfunction. "It's hormonal," they say, as they shrug, both shoulders flexing full mobility. All four physical therapists told me that the condition "must run its course," as if it were a tantrum or warts. My doctor told me, one day, my shoulder would thaw, and I will suddenly be able to reach up to the top shelf or put on a bra without struggle. *That's the ambition?* Instead of science, I get a fairy tale: one day my prince will come, my curse be lifted, my beauty revealed, my iciness melted by love. I will gracefully put on a bra. I only have to wait.

A student tells me about women in refrigerators, the comic book trope also known as "fridging," or stuffing the dead girlfriend of a male superhero into a refrigerator, the specific plot device that shows us a general tendency to rape, kill, or irreversibly disempower female characters in the service of furthering the male hero work. Stuck in the kitchen, one way or another, women are "used," "damaged," "spoiled," then completely expired or fridged. Inside this comic book trope is the culture that created it. The medical field goes on with their doctoring and researching, fridging women's bodies in order to center male ones. In this narrative, my frozen shoulder could be foreshadowing; it could be that I've been changed by whatever men think, or don't, of me. It could be that I'm becoming disposable, one body part at a time. Maybe I'm too much of a minor character to be fully fridged, but my walking around partially frozen reminds everyone of where the story is heading.

Here's a counter narrative: I read about an expectant mother who knits her baby a layette while dosing antinausea pills: a row, a pill, a row, a pill. A friend says, horrified, don't you know that those pills could make your baby be born without arms? The expectant mother replies, "That's fine, I can't knit sleeves anyway." But arms—extended, embracing—are what connect us; shoulders are living bridges between us and the world; desire activates them.

I open a book of poetry and randomly read this line as if it were a horoscope or a fortune: "my shoulders emit pangs of imagined horizons . . . / and lend the reader moisturized wings." My elegant one, my uncrushable one, my panged one, one moisturized one, my shy one, my commanding one.

Long ago, a teacher told me that my greatest strength as a writer, the capacity to inhabit many perspectives at once, was also my greatest weakness. At the time I resented the convenience of this quandary, but it's true, I'm always on-the-one-hand / on-the-other-handing myself. My ambivalence, I came to understand, both embodied the essence of my teacher's formulation and was, in itself, the problem. Opposites often inhabit one another; knowing coincides with not knowing. On the one hand, sexy shoulders are Geminian power parts: hot shoulders for the omosophiliac. On the other hand, we are susceptible, as the French say, to bursitis, rotator cuff tears, and frozen shoulder. The weather scale of womanhood bounces from hot to frigid, slut to prude, and back again, where one persists in and through the other.

Here's another fairy tale about being stuck. Frozen shoulder hurts a lot until it doesn't hurt anymore and then you know it's totally fucked, like a relationship in which you no longer fight or cry together. Mine only hurts now when I try to force it above my head or behind my back, and it hurts at night in bed. It has rendered sleep into a series of horizontal waiting postures. When the pain comes, it radiates like a bad tooth ache and brews nausea. Referral pain shows up in my wrist and elbow, in my neck and fingers. My shoulder is a kind of phantom limb except the limb is still there, all amputated feeling, no function. I know my shoulder is still there because it hurts, not because I can do things with it—because I mostly can't. My shoulder is replaced by the pain of having a shoulder that ceases to be a hinge, useless like a dead thing still attached to its pain.

A suffering woman becomes poetic only so long as she is beautiful, and her suffering is singular, that is, as long as her suffering doesn't implicate us. For example, the plot of the movie *Frozen*: a girl's magic powers to freeze things, unleashed in moments of heightened emotion, isolate her and overwhelm her with guilt after she inadvertently traps her town in eternal winter. We believe in invisible currencies: gods and ghosts, astrology and climate, germs and vitamins, but we do not believe, really, in women's pain. Or like a frozen kingdom, we believe it can be corrected with love. If frozen shoulder weren't mostly a condition of perimenopausal women, we would study it more and know how to treat it. Instead of continuing with an ineffective litany of hope— or a scientific litany of ozone and cortisone shots, physical therapy, acupuncture, chiropracty—I fantasize about a geographic cure. I decide to take a break from treatment and become something else, a tourist. Walking the streets of Paris did at least override the pain and distract me from my search for answers. "Come back when it's thawing," the experts had said, sending me away with cupping bruises like eyespots or areolae sprouting manically across my back and shoulder.

IF TO TELL *all the truth but tell it slant* requires looking askew, I might have been born for this one-sidedness. My lopsidedness easily becomes second nature; the world comes at me aslant and sliding, which is the best way, the most historically appropriate way, to look at the *Nike of Samothrace* at the Louvre in Paris. I climbed the wide marble stairs looking up at her outsized magnificence, dynamic within the vaulted marble ceiling around her. As the exhibit label instructs, I stand three-quarters on the diagonal, my frozen left shoulder to her frozen left wing. To look at her, I tilt back my head, exposing my throat to take in her gorgeous shoulder feathering out into a massive uplifted wing. She towers above the global picture takers, who push ahead holding their cell phones right in front of her, where she visually diminishes. She has no arms because they have been broken off. Head and feet, too. Even though early restoration of the work cast the greatly fragmented right wing as a symmetric plaster version of the original left, we know now, the right wing was higher, slightly smaller, and less detailed. The destroyed wing was remodeled soon after she was found in 1863, but not the head, arms, and feet. Without limbs, she flies off in all directions at once: her wings reach back, her chest forward, her legs press down, her clothing torques like a screw around her. She struggles against a headwind at the same time the wind organizes around her. She moves into it, joining forces. If her whole being responds to the wind's rush and flux, and it does, why do I think of Sylvia Plath's observation in "Edge" that "the woman is perfected" in death, her bloodless, silent body idolized?

Her missing features activate our looking, invite our fantasies. Do we like her better without her head? Without the ability to push us away? Do we read her whiteness as blankness? Her whiteness is redolent of the lady on the box of my first perfume, a gift from my grandmother after months of begging, on my eleventh birthday in 1979. Pictured on the box is a white lady with white flowers spread out like silky wings around her shoulders. This was White Shoulders. The perfume still exists, though Elizabeth Arden, who bought it in 1989, changed its formula. The perfume exists now in name only, which is its most important feature. Extolling the whiteness of shoulders, imbuing the whiteness of white flowers from which it's made with the scent of white supremacy, the perfume's name fuses whiteness synaesthetically with desirability, beauty, seduction.

Some say the perfume was the first American rival of the French industry, but this *Nike* is no rival. Nor is she French. *Nike* means "victory," not rival, in ancient Greek, though she was actually stolen from Greece by the French. Her location under-mines her message. For almost a hundred years, in scholars' imag-inations, the Victory held a trumpet, a wreath, or a ribbon in her right hand, as a symbol of the news she brought back from the war. Then in 1950, the earth coughed up her right hand, reveal-ing an open palm and two intact outstretched fingers, suggesting that she never held a thing. She is simply holding her hand up in a gesture—of what? Of greeting or invitation? Of the open lie of whiteness? She holds out to us the empty hand of victory.

I would not have stood in front of her if my daughter had not had *Nike of Samothrace* on her very short list of must-see works. I had seen this statue the only other time I was at the Louvre, in 1989, but I did not seek it out, and I have seen enough reproduc-tions of it in one lifetime to feel oversaturated. I came pre-jaded to it: its epic contrappostoing; its white marble austerities; its cloth-ing slipping off in voluptuous folds skimming the skin, more nude than naked; its headless inability to look back at us. Why hadn't restorationists felt compelled to remodel her head as they had her wing? Did they romanticize her headlessness, her lack of identity or demand? To the goddess Nike, we come with a long history of looking at decapitated women. We look at women's bodies, dis-abling their capacity to look back at us, to make us feel seen, and to demand that we change our lives. *Nike's* eyelessness instead allows us to look at her solely as an objet d'art, as an unseeing body, present for our pleasure. Paradoxically, I knew, because of the ubiquity of her image in the world, that she would be difficult to see, appreciate or admire, especially in the summer mob and crush of the Louvre.

Yet looking at her now: she corresponds in unexpected ways. Her wings seem to have sprouted when she gave up trying to shoulder the world. It's like the dream in which you suddenly you remember you can fly. As if thrown into the air, you sud-denly realize you are flying. Why have we traded our wings for shoulders, arms, hands? We exchange thrilling freedom, the rush of sky around us, the mind flying off, for precision and intimacy. I'm locked into her airstreams of tenderness and secrecy, her wings flashing out in rage and announcement, until, like a dream, she floats away from me, resists the intimacy I'm assuming. As easily as her cold shoulder folds into my fantasy of identification, it turns into a codified form of empathy I want to betray. Her numbness begins in my phantom shoulder. There, the promise of dislocation flickers. My shoulder is a thing that might at any moment turn to stone or gold or dust or feathers.

With her feet missing, *Nike* looks to me like she is launching herself from the ship's prow, but scholars say this is the moment just before landing. We know this because her alula feathers or bastard wing, equivalent to the human thumb, is extended, intending to slow her down. She is frozen in the process of braking. The prospect of breaking free—shaking off my lockedness—of thawing, suspends me, giddily, with her.

Nike's feather pattern mimics that of a bird except for her primary flight feathers. Greeks depicted and generally understood birds' flight feathers to be spread out evenly, clearly articulated, like a hand fan. In *Nike,* they overlap, bunched and layered up. There is nothing else like it in ancient Greek art. The closest thing in nature is an eagle's wing in molt, the process of replacing worn, old feathers. *Nike's* molting flight feathers say this is a liminal time, a turning over. We know, too, that the wings were painted blue, Egyptian blue set against a blue wind. The marble thins in the center, rendering them translucent in their original outdoor setting, where light and wind become part of how ancient viewers experienced her. The wings might disappear on a bright day; we might see the outline but forget they are there, or we might remember them but not see them, blue dissolving into blue. Even in this stifling room, she is a portrait of wind and transition.

Nike's power comes from her ruffled feathers suspended in a state of being both seen and sheer. Her power comes, not from heroic balance, but from her vulnerability, her withdrawal from the sky. Her power resides in the moment of passage where the past molts, feathers unfix; it comes mid-conversion. I suddenly feel my hormones evacuating like a strong undertow holding me to her stormy mysteries, percolating between war and victory, between victory and its meaning. This is the story that leaps to mind only when my body has prepared my mind to hear it.

To my fourteen-year-old daughter, *Nike* might embody another transition, the promise of sex and independence. Like her, I did not see *Nike*'s cold consolations when I was a young woman. I missed her petrified panic of crossing over: her molting wings, her folds and wrinkles, her furred pulse and pelted chin, her last egg spent, her shrinking, stiffening, desiccating cunt. She hovers over her own otherness, a monument to perimenopausal women, to all the unspoken—unspeakable!—things that happen to women's bodies. We are done with completion. Done with the whimsies of estrogen and spectacle. Done with trying to be beautiful. The wind moves us to do what we want, even as we fight against it, even if it doesn't make us happy. We are winging it now because we made it. We made it through the male gaze. We made it through the fire, out of the spotlight, off the table, around the gender bend, heading into the wilderness of witches, hags, and crones. Looking at her, both seeing and not seeing her, I feel my own visibility strobe, I feel it twilight and sputter as my own wing shoots out like starlight, like a flame throwing sparks, like a sharpening blade, the right weapon for the time.

ICY GIRLS, FRIGID BITCHES, FROZEN DOLLS

A child takes a bite of cold, creamy cake at the New Year's party. Her teeth come down on something hard, and she pulls out of her mouth what looks at first like a pinky bone, but is, on closer inspection, a tiny human figure.

MY GRANDMOTHER IN the retirement home, smiles at me, stirring her tea with the porcelain legs of a Frozen Charlotte doll.

SOME GIRLS PUT Frozen Charlotte spells on witches in the neighborhood; some impetuous girls wait for their own sisters and mothers to turn white and dead. Wildernesses of grief grow up inside them.

MY DAUGHTER READS a novel about an abandoned girls' boarding school on the Isle of Skye: broken chairs where squirrels nest in dark corners, cobwebs in the chandelier, a cabinet full of Frozen Charlottes.

I DREAM THAT on the first day they reopen the beaches, I reach into the undertow and pull up a fistful of the tiny dolls and a few severed heads on their way to becoming stones.

ON AN ISLAND named after an animal that's an old euphemism for snatch: I find hundreds of tiny porcelain dolls, frozen in time. That's a place to begin, on vacation in Beaver Island. I still think the joke is funny: I imagine the island crawling with vaginas: a bevy of big-toothed beavers, a cooperative of cunts, a destruction of pussies, a sororal ossuary of creamy Charlottes. That's how I first encountered the tiny Victorian-era doll called the Frozen Charlotte: huddled together in a bin on a remote, wooded island, a three-hour ferry ride into Lake Michigan. Our rental car was a seatbeltless, unlocked sedan from the '90s with a note on the dashboard and keys in the ignition, waiting for us at dock. Town was a café, a post office, a museum, a church, a grocery and hardware store, and a labyrinthine gift shop, unfolding room upon room of murky curiosities and quirky artifacts of a once-thriving splinter Mormon kingdom. Here is where I would have delighted to find one precious antique doll. Instead, I found a pile of "authentic Frozen Charlottes," porcelain naked girls of about one to four inches, whose features were slightly worn and dirty. None were exactly alike, but close enough to understand they died out due to a minute gene pool. Vaguely defined eyes, nose, and mouth, vaginal mounds, knees and belly buttons—mold seams running down her sides like keloid scars. Each doll is the color of baby teeth, arms slightly bent or folded across the chest, but never jointed—she is "frozen" after all! Her hair is wavy in a pixie bowl cut. Her toeless feet are too rounded or uneven to stand. These dolls could only lie stiff in a bin, on top of one another, a mass grave of sorts.

We like our dolls pedagogical (baby dolls) or aspirational (Barbie or Bratz), letting us rehearse our fantasies and fears of adulthood. Girls understand implicitly that they are either mothers or gods to their dolls, who stand in for coming babies or for their own freewheeling and fashionable womanhood. Wife or slut? the dolls ask us, and this either/or logic is what will have to suffice for choice. No wonder girls are sometimes sadistic to their dolls, biting off their fingers or burning their hair. The obedient doll is the child adults prefer, the favorite child, and she replaces us, destroys our lives, humiliating our originality. We live through her; we punish her in return. But this doll, this plague of Frozen Charlottes, seemed to reverse the script. It might seem sadistic to asks girls to play with dolls that can't stand on their own, but remember Barbie's permanently pointed feet and stature-toppling plastic breasts. She required my small hand around her small waist to hop her from her townhouse to pink convertible because she was designed to remain horizontal, to lay in bed until my hand brought her to the upright life I imagined for myself.

Frozen Charlottes, however, had girl bodies, naked-toddler-on-a-summer-day bodies, unexaggerated and not meant to be dressed in the latest fashion. The first ones were made in the 1850s in Germany, where they were called bathing dolls or naked baby dolls (*badekinder, nachtfrosch*). They floated in water! As they gained popularity, production spread to France and England then America where they stepped into an American ghost story and acquired their American name.

The ghost story keeps coming back to life in new forms. On American soil, "Young Charlotte" is a folk ballad derived from a poem that was based on a news story. The transmutation moves chronologically from New York to Maine to Vermont then everywhere. In 1843, Seba Smith rewrote a minor piece of journalism in verse, "A Corpse Going to a Ball." The true story featured a young woman who froze to death in her carriage, with her fiancé by her side, on the way to a New Year's ball in New York on

December 31, 1839. Here's a taste from the middle of the long original poem first printed in Maine's *The Rover*:

> "Now daughter dear," her mother cried,
> "This blanket round you fold,
> "For 'tis a dreadful night abroad,
> "You'll catch your death a-cold."
> "O nay, O nay," fair Charlotte said,
> And she laugh'd like a gipsy queen,
> "To ride with blankets muffled up
> "I never could be seen—
>
> "My silken cloak is quite enough;
> "You know 'tis lined throughout;
> "And then I have a silken shawl
> "To tie my neck about."

Seba Smith's poem about Charlotte caught on quickly as a cautionary tale. Don't spoil your daughter and make her vain! Don't let your children grow up defiant to sense! The poem's tension between Charlotte's father, who loves to see her glow up, and her mother, the nag, reveals the conditions for tragedy. When your mother urges you to wear a damn coat, bundle up and shut your trap! Fifteen miles is a long way to ride in an open carriage in a silk dress. What parent has not been drawn into this argument? What daughter has not rolled her eyes at the suggestion that she isn't aware of the weather? It's her body! She won't be seen swaddled like a baby! She looks hot in this dress! She wills herself into a vision gliding across the snow. She is so feverish with reckless glee, anachronistic phrases like *catching your death* cannot stick to her. They ride into the storm. When she and her fiancé, Charley, arrive, he leaps out, extending his hand to her. He's momentarily confused at her stillness, "cold and hard as a stone." That quickly, she becomes a monument to pride and obstinacy. Hundreds of newspapers in the next seven years reprint the poem. William Lorenzo Carter, a musician from Vermont, sets the poem to music. For a decade, he sings the popular ballad far and wide, and he was singing it when Americans first saw the hard, white bisque dolls, which they immediately named Frozen Charlottes. The baby doll found her story in America, as a dead teen stripped of her fine clothes, and everyone loved her.

Listening to Ernst Lord's 1966 version of Carter's ballad, "Young Charlotte," I think of all the times I've vividly, involuntarily imagined my daughter's demise. The song's galloping pervasive sorrow carries me, owned and known for the duration. To be a parent is to constantly relive missteps and moments of inattention that could have led to your child's death. Lord stumbles on the words and breaks pitch, preserving the accident of which he sings. Anyone could leave without a coat, anyone could freeze to death, anyone could flub the words. The song keeps coming, but the girl stays frozen, stuck in the accident, the antithesis of Luce Irigaray's "feminine fluidity." Paradoxically, Lord's song feels like it could go on forever, like a spell holding listeners in limbo, both delivering and protecting us from the sadness of endings.

Every beginning to the Frozen Charlotte story triggers another beginning, an endless starting over or falling backward. Each layer makes her story too complete for a regular doll, whose life I would have to imagine and project, whose emotions I could use to explore my own. She came with a singular story and inside that story was another story, and inside that story was a poem, a song, a life, a morality tale masked as journalism. Her story begins also in her whiteness, itself an origin tale that runs through generations, a destructive mythology that idealizes dead women and pretends to come tabula rasa. As the imported doll takes on a local story, shifting and settling in translation, her context branches and her whiteness calcifies. To mistake whiteness for blankness is as dangerous as it is ordinary. Being white is a kind of self-blinding. Being white means not explaining my references; it means my writing might not reveal much about my subjectivity because I strain to even see it as a distinct experience infused with white supremacy. What it means to be white is most opaque to white people. We don't understand it because we refuse to acknowledge the referent, we refuse to see the pathological systems that made us feel superior. "Whiteness, alone" says Toni Morrison, "is mute, meaningless, unfathomable, pointless, frozen, veiled, curtained, dreaded, senseless, implacable." Whiteness freezes us in the moment just before we can know ourselves. We build identities around gaps and ghosts.

Ten years before writing the poem "Corpse Going to a Ball," Smith was the first American to use the word "scrumptious" in print. This is where another tradition intersects with the newspaper account, the poem, the folk ballad. Instead of taking her into the bathtub as the Germans intended for Frozen Charlotte, Americans baked her into a cake. Perhaps the doll recalled the baby Jesus figurine placed inside a cake during Epiphany, a tradition brought to the United States by Basque settlers in 1718. In any case, the practice of hiding coins or figurines in cakes reaches back to ancient times. Plentiful local variations testify to our love of finding creepy choking hazards in our desserts. Or our sublimated desire to eat babies. Or the American tradition from the 1800s of contracting young women to jump out of oversized cakes, a staple of bachelor parties in the 1970s. Surprise! Who doesn't want to bite into Marilyn Monroe's soft, white thighs as if *she* jumps out of the cake, and not a gangster with a machine gun, in *Some Like It Hot?* Whoever finds the tiny doll in a Mardi Gras King cake can bank on a windfall within the year.

Our custom for the Frozen Charlotte is that you drop her into the batter on the first day of the new year. At the time, Americans favored a type of dessert called a charlotte, especially the charlotte russe, a ladyfinger and Bavarian cream icebox cake. You bake or freeze her into a New Year's cake. There is a party. Everyone comes—neighbors, family, friends. There is dancing and merry-

making. You bring out the cake and all the children dig in, hoping
to find the tiny corpse in their slice. A Frozen Charlotte inside a
frozen charlotte is a perfect convergence of sweet cold perfection:
whoever gets the slice with the doll is going to die. Eat as much
cake as you want! Seize the fucking day. Instead of fortune, the
prize is the prediction of your demise within the year. You have
been chosen! Happy New Year!

A YEAR BEFORE my daughter was born, an archeologist on the
Mediterranean island of Pantelleria unearthed a 4,000-year-old
stone doll. Just as much as dolls can be and have been made out
of anything, they can be made *into* anything. Children don't use
dolls only as intended. Part of what makes a doll uncanny is her
lifelike thingness, teetering between foreign and familiar. We give
this thing our own interior life; she is a receptacle of our wildest
and most mundane imaginations. Yet she is not us. A doll's thingness was driven home for me one recent winter night having dinner with our small city's mayor. I sat next to her wife, who had
just donated her early journals to a library's archive of lesbian girlhood ephemera. She told me that growing up, she used her Barbie's feet to masturbate. She told me the story when I asked about
embarrassing moments in her journal, but she said at the time she
did not feel embarrassed, and she even passed the technique on to
a younger girl. Didn't it hurt, I asked, those pointy little feet? She
said she used her underwear as a protective buffer, a kind of condom for her makeshift tool. Barbie's feet were not made for walking; they were made for something far better, erotic transport. I
had missed out.

I try to imagine late eighteenth-century kids playing with dead
girl dolls. I wonder if they got involved with her given story, which
seems too rigged to feel deeply about, or discarded it altogether. In
some versions, Charley returns Charlotte's corpse to her family. In
others, he dies of heartbreak. Sometimes the story ends with them

both in one tomb, an American romance. Some versions end with Charley bringing the "voiceless" Charlotte inside the dance hall, the song's last word echoing Poe's death-drenched "The Raven," published just two years after Smith's poem "never more!" In America, the Frozen Charlotte sold with the sole accessory of a metal casket. Did children play funeral with her? Séance? Did they rehearse death by bringing her back to life? Maybe they conjured the world with a dead version of themselves in it, mouthing their dialogue from a disappeared place. No child believes in their own death; they cannot swallow the most mundane, unbelievable fact of our lives: that we die. For children being dead is like being "it" in a game of tag, a special status, a reversible condition. Young adults even fail to comprehend death's finality, that once dead, you stay dead. Believing that is more preposterous than believing in Santa Claus. When a teenager I knew killed herself, her mother told me that her friends kept texting her dead daughter's phone. As if the daughter might be reached via this portal, this hotline to the underworld, or that the phone itself was part of her body, still living and communicating.

Growing up, the shelves in my room were filled with dolls that my grandparents brought back from their continuous cruises across the globe. Each return came with a doll for me from Russia or Thailand or Australia or Turkey. I was not allowed to play with these dolls. Though I sometimes tried, they had stands and ceremonial clothes that did not come off, and it was never satisfying. They were my white-girl colonial collection, my imperialist trophies, though I never asked for or sought out this collection. Like whiteness itself, they just arrived, a bad-faith birth right. A roomful of display dolls from places I'd never been coincided with my desire for a different kind of doll. This was confusing as a kid. My specific desire was illegible to the adults around me, and my dolls themselves became a way of inhabiting invisibility. I had wanted dolls that my mother objected to for one reason or another: Baby Alive would bring worms into the house, Bizzie Lizzie required batteries, other dolls were too expensive. I had only three dolls to play with, a Holly Hobbie, whose old-fashionedness I despised in the age of Barbie; a Crissy whose red hair grew or shrank back into her head; and a German Skipper doll, Barbie's younger sister who had dark hair and a flat chest and flat feet. I had to go to the neighbor's house to play with regular Barbie dolls. My childhood yearning for dolls must have left a mark on me; as an adult, friends often give me dolls. I never know what to make of it as I don't actively desire them anymore. I have a doll a stranger in Italy insisted I take, one that a secret admirer put in my grad school mailbox, and another a boyfriend gave me, saying it reminded him of me.

The two dolls that I currently treasure, both about the size of a real baby, were also gifts. Unlike most of the dolls given to me by others, these feel like they are mine because of how I acquired them. They sit shoulder-to-shoulder, almost holding hands, like they are happy to have found one another, to be locked in one world together. They do not seem to see me. This animism is exactly what Freud was talking about; dolls give us immediate access to childhood magical thinking. Even though I did not have these dolls as a child, they stand in for the dolls I did have and return me to my girlhood perceptions. My friend Claudia gave me the first, a decrepit old doll with a cracked and peeling face and stripped down to her stained and torn muslin undies. Her best feature is a new voice box, stolen from another doll and planted inside her. When you hug her sad, soiled, falling-apart body, she says the Lord's Prayer with a delightfully prissy British accent. The effect is jarring, eerie, bewitched. Pro parenting tip: find a creepy doll and place it just outside your office door and your child will never bother you while you are working; she will think the entire area haunted; she would rather go hungry, entangled, hurt than approach your door. Claudia gave the doll to me when she had a child because she thought it would be scary to her daughter. I didn't have a child at the time, but never thought to rid my house of scary things when I did.

Beside this doll is my grandmother's doll which I first encountered while staying with her one spring break in college. She had recently moved into a home for widows of army officers. On the train ride there, I scripted elegant answers to the questions I imagined she'd ask me. But she wasn't curious about my classes or my plans after graduation or what I did on the weekends. Instead, I shouted questions at her as we unpacked boxes: a tube of ointment, the end cured around itself, with a 1965 expiration date; bone buttons carved into faces of Japanese gods; a deck of cards with the faces worn off; a bag of fingerless, lace gloves; many jade *figas*; an arabesque patterned saucer to put your cup on while you drank spillage out of the "regular saucer." If she heard my inquiries about her things, she dismissed them: "oh that was so long ago" or "I don't remember." When we scooped the large porcelain-faced doll out of a trunk, it was my last day there. "This was my mother's," she said, sitting the doll on her knee and tenderly smoothing the painted waves of black hair. She said her mother had been the youngest in a caravan of eight families traveling by wagon from California to Lostine, Oregon. When the group had been just days away from their destination, they made camp in an already-cleared rocky lot. Probably it had been used by another wagon train, who had to leave in a hurry, running from an attack (or provoking and then running from an attack). They saw ash, charred sticks, a man's trampled hat, and arrowheads in the dust. At the edge of the clearing was the doll. The man who found it had three children of his own, but he gave it to my great-grandmother because she was the youngest there. Once passed on to my grandmother, she sewed a new torso for it as the original leather had become brittle and stiff. She put on her own outgrown linen dress that she stitched with flower embroidery. My grandmother told me that the doll carried the spirit of another child, presumed dead. The doll's black socks were motheaten to lace. Holding this doll between us had pushed me into a temporal vertigo—we existed together in the chance of time and this doll made us both into girls, daydreaming about our futures. I was desperate to attach my history to the doll's, to be passed this legacy of survival. "That's the story I remember," my grandmother said, "but my mother laughed when I told it once in front of her. She said, 'You've put some words in my mouth before, but I don't know where you got that tale.'" We laughed together because *having an imagination* was then what we shared; the phrase often leveled at me by her own son, my father, as an insult and dismissal. I wanted to find something more of myself in this lost doll, something of what I was becoming, having come from her. My grandmother kept the doll until she died.

THE UNCANNY TAKES as its premise that the estranged begins right at home. *Heimlich* is a word whose meaning develops in the direction of ambivalence, until it finally coincides with its opposite, *unheimlich* or uncanny. Hélène Cixous points out how Sigmund Freud's famous essay on the uncanny is itself uncanny, "less like an essay than a strange theoretical novel." I would call it a ghost story or a tale of trances and residues. The "uncanny" traces back to a concept that psychiatrist Ernst Jentsch explored in 1906 and that Freud elaborated on fourteen years later, merging the concept with Edmund Burke's much earlier theory of the sublime and Otto Rank's fresh exploration of the double or doppelgänger. Freud defined the uncanny as an alchemical juxtaposition of the familiar and unfamiliar, something *strangely* familiar or *secretly* familiar. Something repressed has returned, and along with it our narcissistic overvaluation of our own mental processes, our childhood belief in our own omnipotence. A latent magical power awakes. We thought we were over it, but magical thinking comes back to us. A whiff of terror keeps us spellbound. Spatial and temporal dislocations—the dead teen now a tiny bisque doll forever frozen in her dying hour before the new year—grip us tightly. Frozen

Charlotte throws into question our boundaries between what's hidden and revealed, imagined and real, past and present. What, after all, do we even know about life and death? So much of us can break down, but still survive. Do you believe in ghosts and spirits? The soul? An afterlife or reincarnation? Heaven? Did you once believe?

When I was on Beaver Island, I wanted to buy all the Frozen Charlottes in the gift shop and give them away, but the only person I could imagine appreciating them was my mother. Her eccentricities display themselves in collections and curio tchotchkes—she calls them knickknacks—that choke her walls and shelves. I bought her one. I knew the Frozen Charlotte doll was a morbid gift, but I didn't care. Some gifts you give are morbid and you give them because sadness is your glue. You share a mood, you offer a token of it, an acknowledgment of a dead girl living somewhere inside you both. I've always been a sadness magnet, and my mother's manic depression is partly why. The doll's name recalls the only friend I've ever had named Charlotte, a new girl in sixth grade. I had been a veteran new girl by this point, wearing my awkwardness and terror more like a personality than a situational condition, but Charlotte made "new girl" look glamorous. She showed me the right way to show up. She was beautiful, smart, and looked like she came from the future; her boobs definitely looked like they arrived from late high school. She had moved from Texas where she had some sort of accident involving bleach or maybe Drano that made her tear ducts constantly active. She always had tears in her eyes. Streaming down not as fully formed emotional drops, but a slow leak of tears, a sad song barely audible behind her face, brightening and magnifying her eyes. I forgot about the tears eventually. After that, they covered every lovely thing, the world smeared in a wistful morning mist, a grieving only recognizable to another girl crying or screaming on the inside.

THE FROZEN CHARLOTTE is both a product and a portal. She arrived in time to embody a haunted tale caught in a cultural echo chamber reverberating with other fairy tale characters. Like Snow White, her dying is only a temporary dormancy. Like Sleeping Beauty, she's suspended, waiting, like we all have, for something to happen, for a catalyst to break us out of our sleep. Time stands still, the body suspended like a doll; time in the story makes room for us. This pause is my favorite part, the open expanse of it. We are waiting on the verge of a fairy tale; our hope is a new doll, stiff and lustrous; our recollection is a discarded doll, unlovely and old; our repetition, our continuation, is an indestructible doll that fits closely in our hands and tenderly. The point of the Frozen Charlotte story is that you are not special. You could freeze to death and become a mass-produced figurine that thousands of children covet then neglect. You could become the cheap product of a whole culture in the throes of dead children. Google *Frozen Charlotte* and you will find thousands of images of her. Perhaps without even knowing it, we have already continued living through her.

The doll shows us the fantasy of girlhood, the good girl who loses sight of her goodness as she becomes real. What draws me to the doll is the vague but persistent sense of having lost my true and best self. A feeling of having once been more free, disciplined, attentive, athletic, daring, intelligent, and attractive. My imagination seems cloistered in the before and after, in the uncanny's feeling of remembering something you've repressed, like the ability to fly or your great grandmother's memory. Having once known infinitely more but forgetting it all in the process of living. Perhaps I am remembering a time when I identified so strongly with dolls, I joined their ranks, perfectly fulfilling the needs of others and my own fantasies. I left that person behind in an indistinct and instinctive decision to be alive. I let myself cleave in two, splintering first and second person: a doll and a child, a writer and a reader. I cannot remember a time when I have not chased both a better tomorrow and looked back for my better self. The now comes into focus as an idealized stereovision of the past and future. The doll holds the self on the brink of awakening into a dream realized, a well-worn Romantic motif. Born firmly in the Victorian era, during the age of the modern ghost story (Poe, James, Lee), when the "uncanny" gained its spectral aesthetic currency, the Frozen Charlotte saturates this motif in Victorian structures of feeling. The uncanny slips through the supernatural, and the Frozen Charlotte's popularity begins to die only when Queen Victoria herself dies.

LIKE FREUD'S ESSAY on the uncanny, I wanted to write this essay in two parts, but the doubling keeps proliferating unmanageably, and the stories keep unstacking like Russian dolls. It's as if I can't bear to imagine my own death.

I WAS SURE my mom was the right person to receive the Frozen Charlotte because of her reflexive gallows humor. When I give it to her and tell her the doll's story, she exclaims, "Poor Charley!" Wait, I'm confused. When Charlotte dies, my mom feels sorry for her boyfriend? She surprises me further with sarcasm: "Well, that's cheerful." As a defender of the patriarchy, I might have anticipated her sympathizing with the man and not the mother or the young woman. She is the type, male identified. Never happier than when I give the phone to my male partner to speak with her. That I pegged her as a fan of the macabre without her acknowledgment of it as such is more complicated. After my father died, I asked her about a do-not-resuscitate order; in response, she told me a story about a man who came out of a coma after fifty years. She wants to live at all costs. Even if "frozen" in a coma. At the same time, she competes with things to be the subject of her own story, the narrator of her own life. All the trinkets and things piled up around her remind her that she is not waiting to die because she is waiting to live. Perhaps the Frozen Charlotte throws her formidable will to survive in her face.

The Frozen Charlotte is not the figure of perfection, except in the Plathian sense of a woman being perfected in death. She is the flattened character of social rebellion, the quintessential beautiful corpse. *Arrogance, vanity* the gods cry! Her story keeps reiterating itself, if faintly, as if looking for a companion, another frozen woman. I would like to introduce her to one. Or perhaps she comes back in 2015 as the young woman who believes in the healing power of cold. She works at a Las Vegas spa, where after hours she sometimes gives herself a cryotherapy session. Cryotherapy is deep freeze therapy—which takes place in a chamber filled with liquid nitrogen at −240° Fahrenheit—that deadens irritated nerves and preserves youthfulness. It's a cross between beauty treatment and health care. Clients use it to reduce pain, burn calories, strengthen immune systems, and halt aging. You can get a cryofacial, known by its cutesy argot, "frotox," or you can get cryosurgery (for prostate cancer, among other things). One morning, her colleague discovered her frozen rock solid in the chamber. Chelsea Ake-Salvacion, age twenty-four, became a twenty-first-century Frozen Charlotte. Frozen Chelsea.

We daily see ourselves and others frozen on-screen in awkward mid-gestures on Zoom. We understand our frozen images as the product of unstable connections, which as a metaphor, helps us unfreeze the moment. The COVID-19 pandemic threw us, a little numbed and disoriented, into a time capsule. We had been living as if our neoliberal arrangements were fated or were a force we were helpless to redirect. We thought time would keep ticking, then came COVID-19, the pandemic, the variants, the quarantine cycles. What is the future if it is foreseeable? Is it even a future? If time courses mindlessly around the same tracks, do we call it a standstill, a rut, a waiting period? Some people believe so fervently in the future that they can imagine picking up where they left off after they died. You might know that Walt Disney's body is frozen for some future time when the medical industry has figured out how to restore him, and he can keep creating his empire, an embodiment of the ultimate futuristic movie. Cryonics is a movement, a kind of pseudo-religion that believes in preserving dead bodies at exceedingly low temperatures until a time when technology might give them a second life. Cryonicists endorse a future that doesn't pretend to know where the stakes of death might migrate: Are we dead when our heart stops? When we stop breathing? When we can no longer remember who we are? At the same time, they have a very static idea of identity, one that is tied to the present versions of ourselves, as if culture did not partly fashion and interpret us. It's not easy to look away from the mirrors that culture creates for us. Cryonicists pump the body with a kind of antifreeze to keep it in a suspended state by way of vitrification, a process that turns the body into glass. Collapsing the syntax of fairytale, the glass body waits. At the Alcor Life Extension Foundation in Arizona, headquarters of the movement, hundreds of these glass bodies are heaped underground waiting to be brought back to life. We become dolls with a single story waiting to be awoken into a new world, a sci-fi future written in calligraphy on parchment paper. A memoir on a floppy disc. No one will have the tools to read us.

A young woman had been frozen in a dilapidated family chateau in the Loire Valley for eighteen years, until her husband took his place beside her in a freezer in the cellar early this century. The husband, a biologist who once taught at France's most prestigious medical school and a believer in cryonics, had been planning for his death for over thirty years, but local authorities did not want to supply the electricity necessary for keeping two bodies frozen until American cryonics companies figured out how to bring them back to life. A court authorized the use of force if necessary to gain entry to the chateau and take the bodies to be buried. This is how the dead wife, Monique, became unfrozen in 2002.

In 2020, across the ocean at a marine terminal in South Brooklyn, a long row of fifty-three-foot refrigerated trailers holds hundreds of frozen bodies, dead from COVID-19, until cemeteries and crematories can take them. Tucked into a parking lot, past the fashionable furniture warehouses and next to a crumbling pier building, these makeshift morgues are like enormous tombstones. At the same time, in Tennessee, baby Molly is born from an embryo that had been frozen for twenty-seven years, when her mother was two years old.

If the Frozen Charlotte, a dead doll, a frozen homunculus inside a cake, is a transitional object, the transition is between life and death. Between girl and woman. Here is the temporal frisson: Frozen Charlotte's naked body belongs to childhood, yet her story is that of a grown diva. We have her both ways: a baby and a betrothed young woman. We gloss over the age gap in order to make it work, her body frozen in one time, her story in another. Emblematic of a teenager veering between childhood and adulthood to create a third state, a freewheeling exploration where unknowability quadruples. Teenagers famously carry out a program of inquiry into mortality, entropy, violence, and heartbreak— all notable in Charlotte's story. If we survive, we learn that the world was broken long before we arrived. We choke on our overbearing nostalgia for a past childhood that no one ever inhabited but which we manically invent for ourselves, layering it into our experiences and piecemeal replacing our memories. This revelry of purity is how we simplify ourselves into the ache of cosmic nostalgia, an intimation of vanished glory, of lost wholeness: a memory of an unbroken place, a harmonious world, where we were uncorrupted, full of exacting talents and traits, profoundly promising and promised everything. Time compresses and like more contemporary uses of the uncanny, the doll channels the past in order to constantly refigure the present. The uncanny is an effect of reflection without referent: the mirror staring back at no subject. In the current moment of climate change and pandemic paradigm shift, we might all be Frozen Charlottes whose behavior lags behind our knowledge about the world. We know the planet is freezing and burning, but we don't change our behavior. We know capitalism is killing our planet but do nothing to reverse it. We do not act on what we know. The disconnection is visible all around us.

WHEN IN EARLY middle age my shoulder was clinically diagnosed as "frozen," I thought perhaps that was just the beginning. Could other parts of me freeze? Would my jaw or knees be next? My vagina? Would my whole body freeze solid? What even does it mean to become frigid? You know exactly. Frigid is a word that from the very beginning (1660) has been used to describe a lack of sexual vigor. Yet sometime during the heyday of the Frozen Charlotte, the subject shifted from a man's impotence to a woman's indifference. Frigid describes women's sexuality when not in sync with a man's, and so I wonder what did Charley do or try to do in the carriage that night on the way to the ball? What trauma might have made Charlotte freeze up? In this version of the story, the calm cruelty of Greek myth freezes Charlotte at the moment before sexual violence. Instead of turning into a tree as Daphne had, she turns into a porcelain doll. It is difficult not to think about the frozen body as a metaphor, especially one attached to women. The Frozen Charlotte might be an effigy, or she might be a monument to frozen bodies, frozen time, frozen ideas. As such, frozenness connects women, becomes a salve to historical and personal loneliness. Yet viewing women as a collective tends to erase the individual and viewing bodies as metaphors releases us from responsibility for them.

A bin of frozen figures, stiff and white as bone, manifests when no one wants to play with dead dolls anymore. The final death blows to the Frozen Charlotte come with the war and the flu pandemic of 1918. We no longer wanted dolls to bring death near, we had had enough. It's here in time that another frozen woman

keeps her story locked inside her until the world is ready. Buried
seven feet in permafrost in Alaska for almost eighty years, this frozen woman changed history from the grave. She died of the flu in
Bervig Mission, ravaged, like much of Alaska, by the 1918 flu pandemic. Within five horrifying November days, seventy-two of the
eighty residents of town died; only eight children survived. Officials
paid gold miners to dig a mass grave for them all. One woman
kept the complete virus preserved cryogenically inside her until the
medical field was ready to sequence the virus's genome. We know
a lot about the man who found her. He had been to the gravesite
forty-six years earlier as a graduate student but failed to find the
live virus. As a retired pathologist, seventy-two years old, he went
back alone one week after reading that a virologist was looking
for samples to sequence; his only tools were a pickax, an autopsy
knife, and his wife's garden clippers, which he took without asking. In Alaska, he met the village matriarch who called the mayor
who assembled a village council who granted him permission to
dig. On his fourth day there, he unearthed the frozen woman with
the living virus intact. Before he left, he made two giant wooden
crosses to replace the ones that had almost entirely rotted away in
the graveyard. Later he tracked down the names and ages of all the
flu victims from the village and made a brass plaque to put on one
of the crosses. This man's nickname is the "Indiana Jones of the
scientific set." We also know about the virologists who later used
the frozen woman's RNA to sequence the genome of the 1918 flu
virus. Her body contains the full viral story, something buried that
returns, uncannily, to us: what it is, how it originated, and how we
might prevent future cases and pandemics.

Other than that, what we know about the exhumed body, is
that she was an Iñupiat woman, about thirty years old, and obese.
Fat had protected her organs through the tundra's occasional partial thaws and refreezing. Packed in fat, her lungs were perfectly
preserved, full of blood and H_1N_1. The man who dug her up in
1997 named her "Lucy." He named her not in the tradition of

Inuit people or using one of the actual names from the gravesite. He named her to draw a parallel with another nonwhite female body exhumed by a white man in the name of science. He named her after a pre-human ancestor (once called "the missing link"), found in Ethiopia. Even in death, Indigenous and Black females become colonized and their identities overwritten with Latin names. Remember that other "Lucy," an over three-million-year-old skeleton that shed light on human evolution? She was named after the Beatles song: "Lucy in the Sky with Diamonds." Her message to the world is that all humans have a common origin, yet her name robs her of a specific identity in order to locate her within white culture and the white imagination. This is a problem of whiteness, where white people claim universality, even in the name of scientific "objectivity." In Ethiopia, she is known by her Amharic name, Dinknesh ("you are amazing"), and in the Afar region where she was found, she is known as Heelomali ("she is special"), yet "Lucy" is the name with global household recognition. The Indigenous Alaskan woman should be given a name that reflects her identity and location. At least that. Are we all dolls to them? Do we all belong to anyone who picks us up? No wonder we are icy bitches and frigid wives, no wonder our faces freeze that way. Frozen shut, unable to call out our own stories, our own names, from the grave.

WHEN MY THREE-YEAR-OLD daughter impulsively threw her doll over a bridge into the frazil and slush of the Huron River one winter, I was startled. I briefly imagined she was a cold-hearted psychopath. Then I felt her liberation. We waved goodbye as the doll slowly sank beneath the freezing surface. We had been walking with friends, a father and his young son, who were horrified and ran to retrieve the doll from the river at their own considerable peril. No, I said, refusing to take it back, we are done with the doll.

RIOT AND RUN

A Nylon Counternarrative

We cut our stockings into neck-gaiter masks and hand them out to friends and family. They come colorful, patterned, or opaque. At the beginning of the pandemic, experts said that nylon worked better than cotton because it blocks small particles almost as well as the N95 respirator. Its weave is tight, filtering the smallest particles, and it its elasticity seals around the face. In our effort to flatten the curve, the media tells us to repurpose our nylons, smashing our noses against thigh tubes and mouth breathing, bank robber style. Our breath condenses on plastic like American credit.

AT THE BEGINNING of the twentieth century, the invention of plastic plummeted us into a collective dream, an occult past, a spiritual conjuring, we thought dead, now coming to life in perplexed new forms. We projected ourselves into plastic material's will to change. Yet plastic is, Roland Barthes notes, "the first magical substance which consents to be prosaic. . . . For the first time, artifice aims at something common."

TWENTY DAYS AFTER Wallace Hume Carothers applied for the

"fiber 6-6" (nylon polymer) patent in April 1937, he checked himself into a Philadelphia hotel room and drank a cyanide cocktail. He had been wearing a capsule of potassium cyanide on his watch chain during the synthetic fiber's development, and as a chemist, he knew dissolving cyanide in a citric solution would quicken the poison's effect. His suicide took place at the crossroads of the biological: two days after his forty-first birthday, in the first trimester of his wife's pregnancy, less than a year into mourning his beloved sister's sudden death, and several years before the word *nylon* burst into being. These elements bonded to form a chain of reactions, an exchange of properties. Carothers was prone to wandering off, sometimes for weeks at a time. In those blank moments of his biography, we see him at a distance, walking away, barely visible, on the other side of the river, or tracks, or highway. We know a few things: He didn't want children. He felt bereft in the wake of his sister's fatal car accident. His work environment at DuPont had becoming increasingly unbearable. With the Depression cutting into DuPont's budget, the company officially shifted its expectations for Carothers, demanding he work toward commercial goals instead of theoretical ones. And the more DuPont pressured him to produce commercial applications of his ideas, to move from pure to practical research, the harder he failed to find meaning or inspiration in his work.

THIS ERA ALSO marks DuPont's move away from its original market in manufacturing explosives in an attempt to rid itself of its "merchant of death" image and to avoid antitrust concerns over its stronghold in the defense industry. In doing so, the company transformed the old science of war explosives into the mythical modernity of polymer chemistry. When we say *chemistry*, we mean the effort to turn creativity into money, waste into worth, and sex and death into a consumer good.

CAROTHERS'S PATENT'S APPROVAL—his fiftieth for DuPont—came posthumously. Immediately, newspapers reported that "one of the ways to prepare the new synthetic silk fiber might be to make it out of human corpses" by using cadaverine, a reeking chemical excreted from decaying flesh. Gunpowder and dynamite residue, the traces of wartime death and suicide, it turns out, is hard to shake off. Just like DNA, nylon is a polymer, but instead of cracking the code of life, it impersonates life. At the 1939 Chicago World's Fair, the so-called Princess Plastic, modeling nylons, emerged from a giant test tube, as DuPont's press release sought a rebirth of nylon's image: "wholly fabricated from coal, water, and air" yet "fashioned into filaments as strong as steel, as fine as the spider's web." Using organic metaphors to outdo nature, DuPont heralded the nylon stocking industry and the Age of the Leg. With it came a chemical industry revelation—proof that polymers uniquely could be predicted and engineered—that sparked a vision of a world to come. On May 15, 1940, officially known as Nylon Day (N-Day), five million pairs of brown nylons landed in department stores. They sold out in two days.

NYLONS EMBLEMIZED a technologically rich tomorrow, in step with the dream of air conditioning and television. They evoked the electrified utopian dreams of American empire, extended into the natural world, which would be colonized and perfected through science. Our domestication of the atom meant a Faustian manipulation of creation itself. The life cycle of organic materials no longer mattered: death to silk and cotton, long live synthetics! By returning us to nylon's early affiliation with death, a reminder of how much thanatos is wrapped up in eros, nylons carried a mystique of otherworldly enchantment, a magnetism somewhere between chemistry and alchemy. Before nylons became commercially available, rumors circulated that the tornado carrying Dorothy to Oz was in fact a nylon stocking, filled with earth and blown by a fan, in a miniature scene projected large in *The Wizard of Oz*. True or not, the potent optics of nylon stockings transported us over the rainbow. We marveled at nylon's image of infinite transformation; we swooned for what it might make of us and for us; we titillated at the whiff of death coming off nylon's parade of uniform legs.

AND LEGS THEMSELVES, showcased in nylons, became a kind of uniform of the era. Now that skin could be manipulated visually, white women wanted access to the full range of skin tones, with none of the burden or biases of colorism. Nylons first came in one dark-brown color, but mass production stalled until scientists figured out how to make sheer, "natural" tones. These "natural" colors were, of course, shades of white skin, differentiated in three lines: "beige" for every day, "suntones" for the summer, and "taupe" for special occasions. White women in the 1940s tried to complement their skin color with slightly darker shades that would visually slim their legs and correct skin imperfections. This was not a consideration extended to women of color. Though Black and Brown women wore stockings—decorum required that all women wear something on their legs—they and everyone else understood them to be *for* white women. The men who made these stockings were white, and mainstream American beauty standards valorized whiteness as the pinnacle of feminine chastity and goodness. Nylons demonstrated that white women were so white that they could temporarily adopt darker skin and imbue it with their privilege. They could empty "color" of its despised qualities and keep its physicality, as they embraced a sun-kissed fantasy of endless summer. The irony of putting on darkening nylons, while centering whiteness as a social and political power, lends this story a full dose of the uncanny.

NYLONS HOMOGENIZED the look of all women's legs as if gender itself were a uniform and race were a construct, both of which are true even if we act as though they are not. Science made nylons as it had previously invented race, a white supremacist fabrication. For Black and Brown women, nylons generally whitened their skin. Audre Lorde's biomythography, *Zami: A New Spelling of My Name,* offers a portrait of the culturally loaded object, both seductive and repulsive. At a store in mid-century New Jersey, she fingers the nylons restlessly as her friend urges her to buy them. Ultimately, her rejection of the product is a rejection of its white-washing power: "I hate nylons. I can't stand the way they feel on my legs. What I didn't say was that I couldn't stand the bleached-out color that the so-called neutral shade of all cheap nylons gave my legs."

LORDE'S DESCRIPTION UNPACKS her ambivalence about the fabric's imitation of human skin and a visceral loathing for the intersection of gender-armor and mass production:

> The effortlessness with which those materials passed through my fingers made me uneasy. They were illusive, confusing, not to be depended upon. The texture of wool and cotton with its resistance and unevenness, allowed somehow, for more honesty, a more straightforward connection through touch. . . . I hated the pungent, lifeless, and ungiving smell of nylon, its adamant refusal to become human or evocative in odor. Its harshness was never tampered by the smells of the wearer. No matter how long the clothing was worn, nor in what weather, a person dressed in nylon always approached my nose like a warrior approaching a tourney, clad in chain-mail.

Nylon, according to Lorde, smells like capitalism, stinks like war.

WHEN WE SAY *women*, we mean that white women dubbed themselves protagonists, and they did so at the expense of women of color, who were relegated to side plots as extras or minor characters in the official story. We first saw the solidarity of white women standing together in photographs of nyloned legs in advertising. As they emerged into the light of day, women's legs were always a collective, unified by nylon. The material itself diffused light like the stylized soft focusing of camera lenses rubbed with Vaseline, a common way to photograph women at the time. In nylons, legs became replaced by romanticized images of legs, purloined novelistic scenes of legs posing in the hazy glow and aestheticism of perpetual dusk. Glossy, elastic, skin-perfecting nylons lifted skirts and shifted erogenous zones. Women's legs became the new "erotic weapons," aimed at commanding the attention of men and delivering a deathblow to the Japanese silk trade. DuPont instructed us to "use our buying power for justice [against the Japanese]." But there was no way to guarantee that aesthetics would produce ethics—affect can feed narcissism and beauty can serve violence. As the United States entered World War II, DuPont redirected its nylon production from consumer to military use. With pressure from the Department of Defense, DuPont embraced its history of war profiteering. In 1940, ninety percent of DuPont's nylon went into stockings; by 1942, all of it went to parachutes, rope, mosquito netting, and bomber tires. Encouraged by wartime propaganda and the push to recycle, women donated used nylons to be reprocessed—melted down and re-spun—into parachutes for army flyers.

PICTURE A PARACHUTE malfunction that paratroopers called the "Mae West." The nylon heats, fuses, and refuses to open. Suspension lines then contort the unloosed nylon canopy into the shape of an enormous bra. A woman falling from the sky, hissing and spreading, backlit against the blue. Even in its errors, nylon served projection: a woman who falls from the sky is a concept that refuses to open—a siren, a femme fatale, a Princess Plastic, a Miss Chemistry, a Chemical Girl, a Mae West. These hollow images consume us. Without an animating body, a nylon stocking is an abandoned puppet, a memory gone limp, the saggy shape of a forgotten thought, the seductive spectral shimmering of gender intelligibility. As if women's legs exuded nylon like a pheromone, slipping on a pair meant being marked and molded by the naturalizations of gender.

For women, the nylon stocking was both an intimate garment and the habit of practicing freedom on the ground, striding out confidently to take their place in the public sphere. For a human who wishes to strut or fly, a stocking or parachute is also a prosthetic. In rituals of courtship and warfare, nylon extends the body. Under the sign of "freedom," women strode out confidently into the public eye; men floated through the air into a militarized zone. We grew attached to our supplemented bodies; we libidinized our augmented aesthetics. We embraced our second skins, and the love felt reciprocal. We saw our future through cartoonishly gendered parts. We saw our gender as prosthetic, as the extent to which we go in order to be loved.

IN AUGUST 1945, just a week after Japan's surrender, DuPont launched an aggressive ad campaign for nylon stockings that news headlines succinctly echoed: "Peace, It's Here! Nylons on Sale!" Just as DuPont had created the original N-Day five years earlier, this advertising blitz came packaged as journalism and peppered with numerical precision: eleven pairs for every American woman by Christmas! DuPont slyly transferred its campaign focus from the "miracle material," its mystery easily filled with fear and distrust, to the consumer item itself, the stocking. Loaded with the allure of scarcity and sacrifice during the war, nylons now promised a return to domestic affairs, a reorientation around what white, middle-class women valued. Nylons promised the good life, a return to glamor, to a time that never existed though we wished it had. During the war, the US War Production Board urged churches to destigmatize women attending service without stockings. Now that nylons reentered civilian life, the expectations of ladylike comportment returned full force, revivified by merging style with technology. In this new world, we cannot overstate the social status of wearing nylons. The name itself is a kind of commodity-fetish-meets-science-fiction spell: fashioned from pronouncing the words "no run" backwards then complicated to avoid trademark issues, "nylon" was a consumer fantasy made real by almighty science.

DUPONT HAD MADE its promise. When it couldn't come close to meeting the demand for stockings, women grew outraged standing in mile-long lines for hours. In 1945, 10,000 women gathered outside a store in San Francisco, 30,000 lined up in New York, 40,000 in Pittsburgh: the Nylon Riots erupted. For nine months, shoppers smashed showcase windows; they shouted, punched, pushed, and passed out. All year long, headlines told the news: in Los Angeles, "Near Riot Puts Nylon Sale Off"; in Syracuse, "Nylon Jam Causes Minor Riot"; in Atlanta, "Women Risk Life and Limb in Bitter Battle for Nylons"; in Memphis, "Try All Tricks in Rush for Nylons; Call for Sportsmanship"; in Baltimore, "Girl Collapses; Woman Loses Girdle at Nylon Sale"; in Washington, DC, "Nylon System Set up to Prevent Stampedes"; in Grand Rapids, "Sale of Nylons Brings Riot Call." In September 1945, Chicago detectives ruled out robbery as a motive in a murder case because the perpetrator had left six pairs of nylons untouched at the crime scene. In January 1946, Memphis retailers complained that customers "sabotaged" their coupon system for fair distribution. That same month, the *New York Times* reported "a mob . . . of frenzied women" who "shrieked and screamed ecstatically" as they made their way through a maze made to prevent "the throngs from rushing the counter" to purchase nylons. By the spring, after calling in riot police on a disturbance of 15,000 customers, a San Francisco department store held 10,000 pairs of nylons under lock and key until they could devise a way of selling them without causing harm, and New York was still contending with "mobs of eager women" who "shoved, ran, and even kicked" to snatch a pair. The riots weren't only the surge of white women running into history: this was the jolt of housewives producing their own reality; this was the uproar of working women struggling for recognition; this was a loud crack in the mythological certainty that politics can exist without violence; this was the shattering of representation; this was the cacophony of mattering. Crowds crashed whole shelving systems and stormed over counters, fighting tooth and nail, to snag the last pair. Women had had enough of nothing, and they knew how to get what they wanted. Though for housewives, nylons were a luxury, and for working women, they were a necessity, both groups of women rioted, and their violence underwrites representation as either its motive force or its condition of possibility. They were not going to sit pretty or unpretty, certainly not passively; their collective rampage recalled nylon's grim beginnings, its proximity to death, its weaponization. They wondered at the death required to birth nylons, and during those nine months of rioting, they sometimes wondered what exactly they were birthing. Whatever it was, it felt like freedom. DuPont had built alluring ideas about the future into nylon's molecular structure; women imbued those ideas with a powerful sense of their own agency.

IT'S EASY FOR us to see them pulling hair and pulsing ahead, thrashing like a refrain to which just a few years before they had been kicking their legs in step and smiling. America has trained us to understand women rioting over a fashion accessory as risible.

They are frivolous and spoiled. They are absurd and expensive. Unfolding in a context of consumption, women's anger was made into an especially silly mockery. We see them in this moment like children whose dutifulness has turned disobedient, scratching faces and ripping each other's clothes. We see them scream, and we hear their pent-up sexual energy. At the National Press Club, DuPont showed a film of two women at Macy's wrestling over a pair of nylon stockings while a wide-eyed saleswoman watched in open astonishment. What possessed these women? The men watching at the Press Club thought the scene was hysterical. Instead of a riot, we find a laugh riot. What makes the riots funny, a quirky footnote to "real history," is the qualifier *nylon,* the oxymoronic pairing. We write it off as mass hysteria, a postwar sexual panic. We scoff at women's parody of masculinity, at their misplaced willfulness, at this porn plot waiting to be tamed by police rods. What sort of person riots to purchase an object of their own oppression?

DURING THE WAR, women worked in every stage of production in order to help their husbands and the state. Women who worked for DuPont during the war, dubbed WIPS (Women in Productive Service), were critical to operating nylon plants, for instance. They had already reimagined themselves as something beyond consumers and objects, wives and whores. Women took to believing in their own power even at the expense of understanding the situational contingency of their support. They believed their place in the workforce secured their emancipation, or at least their lasting impact on the market. As the economy reorganized around civilian life, however, women were expected to move from producers to consumers, from an essential to surplus population, without retaining their political feeling. Their labor was effectively "returned" like an inferior product. But unified by dispossession and riding on the highs of postwar optimism, women resisted ceding their economic power. They demanded control of circulation; they knew the "hose men" were manipulating distribution to drive up the prices and maintain an aura of rarity. They had not endured the sexual harassment, patronizing infantilizations, and low wages of their wartime jobs only to be told to step back. Women could run a household and build a bomber; they could manage businesses and farms; they could produce beyond reproduction and what—in making a distinction between paid labor and unpaid, devalued, culturally naturalized domestic work—Silvia Federici calls "the patriarchy of wage." They understood their power, especially en masse, at the very moment we tried to shove them back into kitchens and bedrooms, re-mystifying them as a natural resource.

AS A HISTORIC condition of women, silence is what the rioters struggled against, and it is what erased the record, what we struggle against now in trying to imagine their own accounts. They may have written their mothers or grandmothers about their flashes of rage, their florescent hope. They may have offered their children blow-by-blow accounts of the eruptions. They may have relayed their tactics to their husbands. But were they listening? Did these women embrace or fear the implicit threat of widely reported violence? We like to imagine them plotting together, renouncing the narcotizing effects of passivity around the water cooler. We see them in photographs: a coherence of white women, jamming the streets, congesting the wide aisles, women who could not find room for anyone else on their pedestals. They wrote official letters, they signed petitions, they waited, and they rioted, but their whiteness protected them from being beaten or imprisoned by police. There are a handful of women of color in these crowds and some men, but this fight was most visibly fought by middle-class, white women. Working-class and bourgeois white women might join in solidarity, but in this volley for power, this unimaginable desire for plasticity, for agency, for mobility, for soaring possibility, they kept a tight grip on their capital as white people. As in contemporary movements like the Women's March and #MeToo, white women fail themselves and their goals when they cling to their whiteness; their aspirations leaving them vulnerable to predations of capitalism, its false promises, its recuperation of resistance. Their racism, their psychic investment in the subordination of Black and Brown people, led white women into identifying their potential power in the very forces that sought to keep them in check. What the riots make clear is the price that white women were not willing to pay for their nylons.

WOMEN DIDN'T ONLY want more, they wanted better. Why did these old parachutes suddenly turn delicate and easy to puncture when they got close to women's bodies? If nylon was strong enough for industrial ropes and bomber tires, surely it was tough enough to endure a day at the office or a night on the town. Women's demand for quality as well as quantity was fundamentally about who would run the new economy. It was a rally for a consumer-driven market, against profit-mongering, lying producers.

DuPont had witnessed long nylon lines snaking through cities even before the war, when department stores insisted that nylons be paid for in advance. They had taken note of high nylon prices on the black market during the war. Immediately after the war, they identified a new marketing target, the American housewife, for the ruthless sport of consumer manipulation and price gouging. Maintaining exclusive patent and production rights for over a decade, DuPont understood nylons through their own deep pockets. Women understood nylons through their own plasticity. Privy to the logic of capitalism, women raised eyebrows and hell. They called bullshit on DuPont for deliberately planning obsolescence and suppressing production. Despite an eight-fold expansion during the war (paid for almost entirely by taxpayers), DuPont's nylon production strategically lagged behind civilian consump-

tion. To shift the blame, DuPont pointed fingers at needy working women and greedy housewives. The company actively shamed
women who kept working once men returned from the war. Press
releases blamed the shortage of stockings on "piggish" housewives who were "animated by the most abominable selfishness."
The media and the Civilian Production Administration picked up
DuPont's language and reissued it as headlines, official reports,
and editorials.

As an early pioneer of spin, DuPont engineered public perception. With divide-and-conquer tactics, they pitted women against
each other in oft-repeated corporate speeches. By naming the riot
after a woman's accessory, DuPont undermined its purpose, just
as the Los Angeles Zoot Suit Riots in 1943 addressed something
more urgent and fundamental than fashion. By calling a protest
a *riot*, they delegitimized the political power of women's anger
and action; they turned it into an impulsive, violent consumer
frenzy. DuPont's misogynist campaign denouncing women's vanity and excessive needs made sure nothing would come of their
demands. This was not DuPont's first or last time to turn on their
own customers, claim no culpability, and redirect consumer attention. Recall a more recent high-profile case in point: DuPont's
decades-long coverup of the lethal toxicity of Teflon. DuPont
wrote the book on corporate deception of the public. Right after
World War I, federal investigators charged DuPont with price fix-
ing and violating antitrust laws. In response, DuPont spun a patri-
otic yarn about fair market competition that newspapers printed
almost verbatim. Through one scandal after another, DuPont's
vigorous publicity campaigns landed their press releases on the
front page of newspapers that they owned. In 1926, when word
got out that DuPont's dyes plant was manufacturing poison gas,
a highly toxic product that killed the people who made it, com-
pany-owned papers reported not a single company death. As
with Teflon, DuPont intentionally covered up their own complicity for years. In 1959, when their newly minted polyethylene dry-

cleaning bags suffocated fifty children, DuPont blamed careless parents. In addition to owning many local and national newspapers and their own magazine, DuPont aired a popular anthology radio series, *Cavalcade of America*, once per week during prime time. DuPont hired blue chip writers to produce scripts that were read by leading actors. These dramas propagandized DuPont as a leader in humanitarian progress through technological innovation. Women's lives in particular, DuPont pledged, would be freed from household tyranny. On N-Day, an entire episode of *Cavalcade of America* was dedicated to a fictionalized interview with a "typical" housewife about the wonders of nylon. DuPont's campaign to keep women happy at home relentlessly extended their commitment to less ironing, better kitchen utensils, and garments that were easier to clean. The dream was a more opulent and easily maintained cage. All that paternalism, of course, had consequences when women demanded a say in controlling production and distribution.

WOMEN HAD GIVEN their nylons to be repurposed into parachutes for men, but in the process of returning these instrumentalizations of gender, the system double-crossed them. When we say *nylon*, we mean the plasticization of women's bodies, encased in the first fully synthetic material, which refigured women both as artificial objects, rigid and timeless, and paradoxically, as unstable fabulations, capable of shapeshifting on a whim. DuPont's effective mixed messaging, percolating with male anxiety, reifies this doublethink understanding of women as both uppity gals who forgot who's boss, and foolish little ladies who don't know what they're doing. Either way, the solution was clear: women's unruly bodies and desires urgently needed management. By coopting the public narrative, DuPont turned the homogeneity of the chorus line into an angry chorus of mass hysteria. But if the Nylon Riots remade a state of war in the department store, it also refashioned the spectacle women had been made to become. Women's clothes historically inform the way we walk and its meaning; nylons gave women a catalogue of walks. The new visibility of women's legs moved them into their place in the public sphere. It gave women a deeper commitment to mobility, action, and freedom, and it gave them something to stand on. These women rioted for the idea of plasticity, for imagination and movement; they called upon a common language to do so. We understand them when they shove and shout and smash things up, desperate to get what's theirs. We recognize their bodies, seized by history, bent on self-determination. What is self-determination made of? It is fully synthetic. In the mid-twentieth century, women had imagined themselves into technicolor, easy-care futures. And over whose dead body were they going to recede back into the dark corners of their tidy houses?

DURING THE RIOTS, nylons began to appear in the news in yet another context. Women turned up dead with nylons tied tight around their necks. In over a dozen articles in the *New York Times* between November 1945 and May 1946, the murder weapon of choice was a nylon stocking. At the crime scene, a man who shot himself after strangling his wife or lover might be a corpse in the same room. Some reports feature what jewelry the dead women wore and who found them. In one case, women in prison loaded one foot of a nylon with a jar of cold cream to beat a female prison guard to death. They were trying to escape. Recalling nylon's material death drive, its early proximity to its inventor's suicide, the cadaverine rumored to create nylon, their mutations into instruments of war, and DuPont's legacy as a gunpowder and dynamite manufacturer, these deaths amplify women's objecthood. A beautiful corpse, or at least a well-adorned one, chokered with *the* contemporary symbol of modern liberation: what did that give evidence to if not the backlash against women's autonomy?

THE WORD *RIOT* was from the beginning a domestic agitation or a sexual act. In the twelfth century, it was also a noise, a folly, idle chatter, or waywardness; it was moving in and out of the house. Even in its meanings, it was disobedient. It wore a nylon over its face as it robbed us of our senses, and it wore a nylon on its legs as it walked freely into vagrancy and loitering laws, informal policing practices and unofficial applications of laws that kept women off the streets. A "man in the street" is a synonym for the citizen, voter, or everyman; a "woman in the street" is a "woman of the street," a streetwalker, a.k.a. a sex worker. Too many women in a house cause that house to legally be labeled a brothel.

OUTSIDE, THE NOISE of gathering women overflows quickly and turns into eros. It leaps into the story of a moral crisis and sexual panic: women "sirening across town." It resolves in paternalism and discipline: men "sirening across the town" (Gwendolyn Brooks). A riot gets dully measured against effectiveness (what did it change?) and the settling of accounts (who won?). But as with that other definition of *riot*, we follow the wrong scent. In hunting, to run riot means to run after the scent of something other than the prey. It wasn't the nylons, or not only the nylons; women wanted to hold on to the power to walk around, to make noise, to be angry and heard.

AFTER 1200, the noun *riot* is "debauchery, extravagance, wanton living"—from the Old French *riote,* a "dispute, quarrel, (tedious) talk, argument, domestic strife" and from Latin *rugire,* to roar—it is anything but accommodating and quiet. For as long as anyone can remember, *riot* has also been a euphemism, of uncertain origin, for "sexual intercourse." In the imaginary OED of women, *nylon riot* means a counter-erotics; it means a death-saturated desanctification of time; it means to reject cathartic closure and

posit instead the limits of the knowable in historic moments of
sociopolitical unruliness, and with it, the liveliness, the aliveness
of possibility.

HAD THE NYLON riot's meanings proliferated and not been stopped
by journalism siding with industry and government or strongarmed
by capitalism; had it not been rewritten by male laughter, nervous
and furious, "indelible in the hippocampus," as Christine Blasey
Ford characterized it in her testimony, we might still be drawing
on its reserves, correcting its oversights, calibrating our gains, and
re-steering its momentum. In other words, if white women hadn't
written Black and Brown women out of the story, and if men
hadn't written off women in the histories, we'd live in that real
"better world" induced not through science but through justice.
The etymology of *riot* tells us something we already know, even if
the knowledge has been culturally suppressed. Despite historical
perceptions, women are often catalysts; they are initiators of rebellion and first actors of riots. We don't know this because patriarchy grooms us to trust its authority, which centers and valorizes
men in the official story. We don't know this because any assembly
of women prostitutes itself to the image of social contagion. Mobs
of women might sweep bystanders into their libidinal chaos, their
mental and medical diseases, their public displays. But, bitches,
will we believe it? What we are encouraged not to know about
women, a patriarchal unknowing, becomes part of the history of
disbelief and trivialization of women's anger. We face this combus-
tible past knowing full well we cannot hear the unheard but doing
it anyway. All the stories never told rush into our mouths, all the
philosophies and songs, all the refusals and fantasies, open ways
forward. We find a way, "working out the vocabulary of silence"
(Muriel Rukeyser), which we hear like shockwaves after a blast
and we feel the reverberation, the repeating echo of women striking back, of new meanings pointing toward new beginnings.

THE RIOT PLUMMETS us into a collective dream, a heritage of fury we thought was dead, coming to life in perplexed new forms. We project ourselves into the riot's material will to change. Yet the riot is the first magical action which consents to be something common.

NOTE: VIOLENCE AGAINST women is continuous, making women shut up and stealing their narratives. This essay displaces the authority of my mostly male sources, who I do not cite as a point. This counter-narrative breaks with the official logics of those sources and challenges our notion of what constitutes a story worth calling "history," or a perspective we might want to take with us into the latest rage.

ALL THE WOMEN I KNOW

A Collaboration with Laura Larson

Mariana

No woman I know tells a story about her grandparents, Wilbur and Maude, though she can't say for sure if it's true.

No woman I know says Wilbur came to visit the family in Pasadena long after the divorce. He said Maude had used a hickory stick while he was away, during the time she was secretly divorcing him.

No woman I know says that's what they did before coat hangers were invented. As if hanging clothes were a secondary use.

No woman I know suspended for an instant between a tree and a window.

No woman I know says that visit was the only time Wilbur came to see his son, her father, Maude's only child.

No woman I know says Maude claimed desertion though Wilbur was only away on business, and they were in touch.

No woman I know says Maude announced their divorce in a German-language newspaper while he travelled as a livestock broker to make ends meet. Imagine his surprise when he returned to the sudden end of their marriage.

No woman I know looks to the endless sky, blowing on and on, an unfolding infinity of male surprise at all the things ending right now.

No woman I know dies of boiling baths and the longest knitting needles she could find.

No woman I know dies with the words *mifepristone, misoprostol,* and *Cytotec* handwritten on a piece of paper in her front pocket, hoping she won't forget to take it out before she washes her clothes.

No woman I know dies of burning hot bricks on her navel, because it was worth a try.

No woman I know dies of the steepest staircase around and a tea of tansy, black cohosh, thyme and rue.

No woman I know looks at the vacancy between two houses.

No woman I know says Maude's mother died after ovary surgery at age thirty-eight, leaving four young children.

No woman I know imagines hugging those children hard to console them while feeling mortified and repulsed by them having no mother.

No woman I know feels herself slipping through an hourglass.

No woman I know tries to imagine her body growing a collection of fingers and another set of nipples, a whole new head.

No woman I know can remember Wilbur, but there's a picture of her sitting on his lap.

No woman I know ever saw him again and thinks he's buried under an empty sky in Colorado.

No woman I know is from a long line of abortion-getters.

No woman I know says Maude went back to school, wrote a thesis on women in religion, and became a firebrand preacher.

No woman I know shrugs at her own unspoken afterthought, a gesture she inherited from her mother.

No woman I know asks if I think Wilbur came all that way for anything other than a late attempt to discipline and humiliate his ex.

No woman I know leaves space for someone to say something. (Say it now.)

No woman I know, now absented, becomes herself.

WHEN PEOPLE ASK me how we met, I tell them the story, set at a poetry event in New York City where we were both reading, though there are parts of it I always leave out and parts I sometimes leave out, depending on who is asking. In my story of how I met my partner, I never tell people that I was pregnant and that I was going home in forty-eight hours to take the RU-486 that I was not yet pregnant enough to take. When I tell our story, I follow a pretty chaste script because it was absolutely chaste, but not for my lack of trying. When he invited me back to his hotel room to watch old movies, that's exactly what we did. Frustrating and charming in equal measure. It goes without saying that I had been conditioned to understand this invitation as code; men have the freedom to speak directly when they want to, I guess, but we are required to understand the possibilities. Back in his hotel room, his best friend called to make sure he wasn't doing anything he might regret, and I used my cigarette to burn a hole in the cover of his book of Vallejo poems. I don't remember what we watched. Since we were put up by the poetry event organizers, my hotel room was directly below his, and I went back at some point and imagined him above me, which was funny, but not so funny that I didn't masturbate.

That weekend, I also did not tell anyone I met that I was pregnant. I had been having occasional sex with my ex. That we hadn't been more careful made me vaguely ashamed and feministly ashamed of my shame. This was not my first abortion rodeo. Some people at this point will say there is no excuse for having more than one. I've heard it many times when people do not know I am that wanton hussy. We give women a one-abortion allowance. Any more seems excessive and pathological. And yet, even if you spend most of your nubile years not-pregnant, even if you regularly use birth control, you can still manage to get knocked up a couple or three times. After all, I had regular sex for over thirty years—10,950 days—before menopause kicked in. They say it takes 10,000 hours to become an expert. In the meantime, mistakes happen. In this spirit, I had a conventional abortion at age nineteen, nearly a virgin, in Pennsylvania; a D&C at age twenty-five, after an endocrinologist told me I would have a hard time getting pregnant, in New York City; then a pill-induced abortion at age thirty-four, single and divorced, in Michigan. Each time with a different partner, all of whom involved themselves in the process. Perhaps we don't recognize the men in those waiting rooms because we think abortion only happens to half of us. Yet the teenager I first had sex with came with a past summer romance that had ended in an abortion. He carried his guilt, profoundly transformed into tenderness and care toward me. I never had to ask him to use a condom or even if he had one, a courtesy that did not prepare me for sex with other men. Because ultimately, those of us with reproductive capacities are on our own. My aunt recently told me about my great-grandmother who "used a hickory stick" before she divorced the father of her son (who would become my grandfather) and moved to another state.

When young men in my creative writing classes turn in pro-life propaganda fiction or young women write poems about fetuses brutalized by doctors, I remember the first anti-choice campaign I stumbled across on campus. When I asked, one of the self-righteous assholes from out-of-state handed me their literature, which exactly mimicked the University's font, design, and logo. It was raining, and I took my glasses off to read pulled quotes about freedom from a Civil Rights leader. I must have dropped them as I lost my shit, shouting and storming past the looming photos of dead fetuses, but seeing only images of dead women. I could not see past my own horror, and I realized I would need more than blind rage to fight this cannibalizing of the language of social justice. Despite my first-hand encounter with righteous language stolen for repressive purposes over twenty years ago, I was caught off guard in the next wave of copycat tactics. Now when I drive past anti-vax protesters who carry signs that say "my body, my choice," the slogan of the so-called "medical freedom" movement, I'm reduced to stammering "really, motherfuckers?" over and over again with steam coming out of my ears. At the very moment record numbers of anti-abortion bills keep clogging the courts, parading their bad faith "compassion" in "a woman's right to know" legislature and "heartbeat protection," this *détourning* of pro-choice language is clearly designed to shut me down and shove me aside. Same as the "vaccine victimhood" narratives, their common refrain "me too," and the talk of "accountability" and "consent" come straight from the megaphones of the women's movement. Perhaps a way to understand this appropriation is that it is not the men, or not *only* or *all* the men, but the white masculine body that presumes itself to be ground zero.

IN COLLEGE, I wrote about my first abortion, and later—much later—my teacher asked if she could include my essay in an anthology on "badass women." She had saved my smudgy dot-matrix-printed essay for my entire reproductive life. I didn't have a copy of it, didn't even own a computer when I wrote it, and rereading it mortified and exhausted me. Back then, I had one literary trick: the dramatic over reveal, an in-your-face candor that acted as a smokescreen for self-examination. You might think that's how this story began, and you might be right. Back then, I was also willing to make myself into a victim because I had clearly been a victim. We might now call my posture a "post-victim" victim, claiming victimhood while at the same time rejecting that gender-specific vulnerability. And though I knew something of the systemic injustices that shape the lives of girls and women, I could not imagine my own powerlessness. I could not imagine that I did not bring it all on myself. I felt myself to be powerful, wild, and free. It's true that none of my decisions to have abortions were very painstaking, and none of the procedures had profound or lasting physical, financial, or psychological effects. But the weight of what my college essay leaves out crushes me with its trauma-conditioned self-regard. What it needs, what I needed then, was to acknowledge the epidemic of sexual violence and the concomitant struggle to matter that women face every damn day. Stories do not allow us to see everything at once—they give us a voice, a fleeting perspective, a framed view. No woman I know will tell a single story as if it's the only one. How do we inoculate our narratives against self-evident language and doublespeak? Make it not slip like a hand up my skirt, "sweetheart," "darling," "honey"; make it think, make it care, make it mean.

Dani

No woman I know can remember how it began or when.

No woman I know begins again and again, each time.

No woman I know and the world not quite awake and too tired, if I were dead tired.

No woman I know leaking a soft growl, like whistling to fend off fear.

No woman I know is an infinity or even half of one tattooed on her neck.

No woman I know in a state of permanent emergency.

No woman I know has snake eyes at the top of her snake spine and owl eyes in the back of her head.

No woman I know constellates visions, signs, emergencies.

No woman I know crawls out crumpled, sleep lines on her hands, wrinkled clothes in dappled light, script spilling all over her skin.

No woman I know trying to tell you something you cannot read.

No woman I know has a siren in her throat.

No woman I know has an emergency alert down her throat.

No woman I know carries a fork when she walks her dog after dark, imagining the stranger she will have to stab under starlight.

No woman I know fits the description.

No woman I know hurrying across the street.

No woman I know could feel more lonely after.

No woman I know was alone on the swings when it happened.

No woman I know stages her own emergency. Not here. Not like that.

No woman I know needs to hear it today.

No woman I know wants to laugh along with the joke, but does anyway, a slight permanent hiss between her teeth.

No woman I know can read the writing on the wall or face it or find the hidden wall behind the foliage.

No woman I know understands what she is up against.

No woman I know has an emergency greater than no-emergency, none greater than the normal emergency of her own body in the world.

Sandra

After Lorna Simpson's *Head on Ice* series and using language from 2021 testimonies of the first eleven Jane Does in the lawsuit against the handling of their sexual assault cases at Eastern Michigan University.

No woman I know got ready with her sisters.

No woman I know went to the party with her cousin.

No woman I know went to the party already buzzed because she was aware of the dangers of drinking at a frat party.

No woman I know snuck out of her parents' house and got into his car.

No woman I know fell on the way there, hitting her head on the curb.

No woman I know kept dancing with her friends at the party.

No woman I know became separated from her friends when she went upstairs to the bathroom.

No woman I know went with him to his room because she had already known him for a couple years.

No woman I know agreed to wait for her friend in the living room, but was escorted to a bedroom, where a man locked the door behind them.

No woman I know felt ice needling her face, her body being crushed by snow falling from giant firs.

No woman I know only wanted to cuddle during the movie.

No woman I know only wanted to play cards by candlelight.

No woman I know felt something in her chest freeze when he called her a tease and a prude.

No woman I know saw his friend blocking the door.

No woman I know saw herself from above, as if looking down through a glacier.

No woman I know pinned and flattened like a blue shadow on the bed.

No woman I know felt her shirt being lifted as he took a picture.

No woman I know splintered or crystalized on the spot.

No woman I know felt her body being lifted into the air like a child.

No woman I know felt herself being pulled by her ponytail as if it were a leash dragging her back into the room.

No woman I know felt his hand palming her head like a basketball.

No woman I know felt like a puppet being jerked into positions.

No woman I know upon information and belief, when she realized his uncle was the police chief.

No woman I know trying to breathe makes her mind blank, as smooth as snow throwing off tiny rainbows like alerts where no one ever walks.

No woman I know feels trapped under him, inside an iceberg, shifting out of time.

No woman I know under the ultramarine light, the cobalt blotches hardening around her.

No woman I know says she wants to go home.

No woman I know with icicles for vocal cords.

No woman I know thinking of her mother to keep herself in the before.

No woman I know slows herself down like hypothermia, like hibernation, like whatever it takes.

No woman I know cannot move as he continues to squeeze and slap her breasts.

No woman I know cannot pull her underwear and pants back up.

No woman I know walks back to her dorm alone and freezing without her coat.

No woman I know agrees not to speak of what had happened.

No woman I know nods when he asks, "You okay?"

No woman I know still waiting for the shock of sun on her skin.

No woman I know tries to recognize the selfie she took as she got ready that night: her eyes sinking into inky laughter.

No woman I know closes her eyes as if she could stay frozen like that in her own memory.

Marissa

No woman I know can picture the room where she was that day. *Is there a window, curtains catching wind and light?*

No woman I know draws a blank when she tries to imagine it. *Can you draw the floorplan?*

No woman I know holds her breath when she retraces her steps into the scene. *Is there a yellow bed or a striped sofa you can arrange into a story?*

No woman I know holds the room down inside her, holds it under her skin, suffocating it.

No woman I know feels herself freeze. *Was it cold enough to see your breath clouds blot out the room?*

No woman I know keeps whiteness in her sight. *Is there something you can photograph and bring back to show me?*

No woman I know was even in the room though the smell of flowers lingered. *Was anyone there with you?*

No woman I know where nothing bleeds and your fist dissolves in the flash bloom.

No woman I know wants to live in your glaring revelation, your certain clarity.

No woman I know used to be glad to come home, before she never left.

No woman I know feels free to wander in the photograph.

No woman I know feels easy in this eternity.

No woman I know has seen too many films to know better.

No woman I know wants to turn off the soundtrack completely, especially your voice that keeps coming even when you aren't around.

No woman I know stopped a migraine in its tracks.

No woman I know can make something in her mind become something in your mind.

No woman I know walks out of that room.

No woman I know carries her girlhood, her mother's and her daughter's, one laminated over the other, until she vomits.

No woman I know wants you to use the horror of her childhood against her.

No woman I know thinks your hand slipped.

No woman I know is light touching paper.

Lucille

No woman I know with all her doors and windows open and her back to the world.

No woman I know trying to live as if it were morning.

No woman I know skywalks into the picture and paints herself out of it.

No woman I know on acrylics and MasterCard fraud.

No woman I know on hash and alone in her dreams.

No woman I know on Paxil and Polyxo, a Naiad of the Nile, a daughter of the river god, and the mother of twelve daughters, all of whom murdered their husbands on their wedding night.

No woman I know to feel herself floating.

No woman I know to feel herself dripping like a popsicle down her own hand.

No woman I know takes a heavy dose of yoga and gouache.

No woman I know on pandemic-time and premature death.

No woman I know even if in timelines.

No woman I know even if in epigenetic memory.

No woman I know even if in encaustics and involuntary memory.

No woman I know in the Reddit thread turns on us perversely or vanishes when we look away.

No woman I know quits mail and deletes Twitter.

No woman I know swallows Tylenol and Alcyone, a star in Taurus.

No woman I know on donkey dust feels she is made of stardust.

No woman I know sees the starlight that has eaten her.

No woman I know falls asleep as soon as her head hits the pillow.

No woman I know goes viral as she sleeps.

No woman I know rates her sleep on the five-star rating system.

No woman I know titles her days or calls them "untitled."

No woman I know with a zygote and eyes like dying embers.

No woman I know prescribes herself to try harder.

No woman I know pulls a reason from her head and leaves a note in large printed letters on her pillow.

No woman I know on radio dramas and Adderall.

No woman I know on tungsten and Robitussin.

No woman I know, her two stories overlapping, lapping at each other like waves: the morning the mourning; the pain the painting.

No woman I know gulps ayahuasca and Calypso, which means "she that conceals."

No woman I know washes it down in the shower.

No woman I know emptying her feed.

No woman I know like that scene in movies when she opens the fridge to find only a few cans of Bud Light.

No woman I know on Sexton and Plath, drawing herself back to life.

No woman I know on strychnine and cartoon heroines.

No woman I know on hormone replacement and burner accounts can ever get what she wants and what she has and what she wants.

No woman I know on peyote and paranoia.

No woman I know though we like to think of her swimming in the wind, dancing in the room, flowering out in the morning.

No woman I know shimmering like a photograph in its bath.

No woman I know on Nyquil and Ryū, a dragon that eats dreams underwater in a red coral palace.

No woman I know on the other side of the ocean, waving.

No woman I know reversed inside our unmeasured eye.

No woman I know all the way in the other hemisphere, standing upside-down in a human shape.

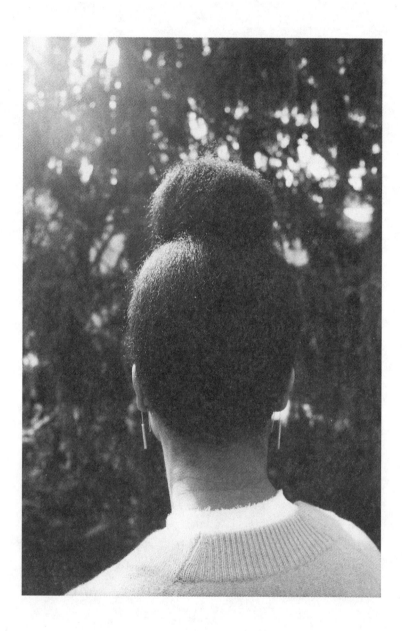

Natascia

No woman I know walks out of the dark building into a blinding headache.

No woman I know with a cracked phone on three percent.

No woman I know hurrying home to change her tampon.

No woman I know between work and home slips into a basement story and is never found again.

No woman I know having just washed her hair.

No woman I know wearing a perfume first made in 1834 disappears from the factory.

No woman I know cuts through branching shadows until she doesn't exist.

No woman I know disappears into yawning or atrophied hours.

No woman I know has an instinct for it, an aptitude for being seen and going invisible as if by her own will.

No woman I know disappears herself into TikTok.

No woman I know dissolves into the scenery of her married life.

No woman I know disappears into a couple people she used to know.

No woman I know disappears into a small round stain on her raincoat.

No woman I know wants her name written on a red balloon and tied to a lamppost or sharpied on the back of a flattened Amazon box and held up in front of city hall.

No woman I know has a referral for this shit.

No woman I know in the waiting room at the time of this writing.

No woman I know loses herself in a good mystery.

No woman I know disappears into books about disappearing women written by men but hears nothing about the real women who drop out of their own lives.

No woman I know enters the murderous sentence unaware.

No woman I know is perpetually replaceable.

No woman I know is waiting to disappear the instant she passes through your feed, untraceable like a mood, like disgust that flashes almost imperceptibly across your face.

No woman I know waiting to disappear hears that her lawyer died.

No woman I know waiting to disappear told her grandmother she was on her way to the bus stop.

No woman I know waiting to disappear holds her tongue.

No woman I know waiting to disappear is white enough to arrive.

No woman I know is waiting to disappear into his shushing.

No woman I know waited as a child to become extinct.

No woman I know circles around the site of her future vanishing, looping like a thought that burns a hole in the brain, an aperture that cannot be closed and keeps letting in light until she no longer shows up.

No woman I know waiting to disappear into a gaze like a lit fuse.

No woman I know and what she fears grow old together.

No woman I know comforts herself by terrifying herself.

No woman I know waits to be found naked in a pile on the floor.

No woman I know passes through her own mind like a thought she will later forget.

No woman I know disappears into several possible aliases.

No woman I know is full of the world.

Dionne

No woman I know grew up in a folktale in Florida.

No woman I know worked as a maid, waitress, manicurist, secretary, and nanny.

No woman I know lied about her age in order to enter high school at twenty-six.

No woman I know wrote her own story through that of another woman.

No woman I know entered the party flamboyantly sailing a scarf over her shoulder and shouting out the title of her play.

No woman I know, when it turned out she couldn't type, passed herself off as a princess from a tiny country on the other side of the ocean.

No woman I know studied her way into confidence.

No woman I know went back to talk to the people of her hometown though by then she had forgotten the language.

No woman I know gathered their stories to prove she had not forgotten.

No woman I know listened to her family pass salt-and-pepper worlds through their mouths.

No woman I know with their sayings swaying like generations of women sobbing and laughing, hellbent on houseboats.

No woman I know in snapshots staring loudly through the band's tangled music.

No woman I know with sentences for manifesting herself out of the haint-blue skies and porch ceilings painted that way where the weather was always under discussion.

No woman I know shaped shards of talk and memory into stories that left out the sour smell of terror.

No woman I know refused to write about accusations, exploitations, or condescension; she conjured the future she wanted.

No woman I know, after being arrested, contemplated suicide but slowly came back to life on a long sailing trip.

No woman I know made a point of not needing what she could not have.

No woman I know tended to marry or not marry men, enjoying them while never relying on them or missing a beat in her work.

No woman I know finds herself in characters who keep finding their way through the muck.

No woman I know pieced together a way of being that may once have existed.

No woman I know with all her sentences burning like black candles in glass jars.

No woman I know wrote about the longleaf woods so that nothing would root her in one place. She wrote about a fox there so that it would not eat its way out of her.

No woman I know wrote about the horizon so that she could pinch off the biggest thing ever made and wrap it around her neck like a sapphire necklace, like a saffron scarf, not like a noose.

No woman I know, no matter how far her sentences go, with the horizon always ahead of her.

ONE THING I didn't say before is that my frozen shoulder began with my fervent snow shoveling during a polar vortex. We had received a ticket for not shoveling the sidewalk in a timely fashion the week prior, though I live with a man from California who hardly waits for the snow to stop falling before he's out there taking care of things for the whole neighborhood. It's still a fun novelty for him, or so I like to tell myself. I was going to show the city and the California boy how to shovel the shit out of that new snow. And I did. And my shoulder was never the same again; even after it came back to life, it felt like it might have been replaced by a replica. My shoulders had been sisterly, but now they are like strangers. My left shoulder, all amnesia and awkwardness, moves in uncanny approximations of the right one. The whole body takes sides. The whole body is a face.

WHO HASN'T THOUGHT when looking at a photograph of themselves: *Is that really how I look?* There was a time when a portrait photographer could hand you someone else's face, and you'd never know it wasn't you. As you looked into the stranger's face, your eyes slid and widened like liquid sliver; the shape of your mouth warped, mirroring. Sure, you had caught your reflection every now and then, but you did not own a compact, a full-length, an entry hall, a medicine cabinet, a silver-backed, a concave or convex. You looked into dirty windows. You did not carry a camera around in your pocket, but you wanted to prove that you existed, so you went to the photographer. And the portrait you're eventually handed gives you access to your own buried happiness and aggression. It gives you a gait that gets you everywhere early. You are quicker to laugh, too, after noting your own undying glow, and people love your laughter. You carry around this self-image like a filter or a charm against your own ugliness. Looking like that, you can say or not say anything, and no one will object. You could walk right into the future. Because, did women even really exist in the past? You had been invited, you clicked the box that said you were coming, but you failed to show up. Wait. Why did women invent the future? Ha! Why did the woman cross the road? Ha, ha! What did she say when she entered the bar? Ha, ha, ha! You keep thinking of the joke until it's too late to tell it—the party is over— and you had forgotten the punch line anyway. The punch line is that you retain a mental image of your face that no longer matches the face you must wear. You want to tell yourself, *just stop, do not continue like this.* You are growing new fontanels in unspeakable places, and it's hard to tell front from back anymore, melting neck and jaw from the molten dorsal thorax pushed up and around your bra line. No matter, you remember what you used to look like, and you carry it around like an absorbed fetal twin— the wise one, the strong one, the funny one, the one too good for this world. Maybe it's the one you aborted. Maybe that face was your social media profile, the face you chased trying to have a good day or a speedy recovery, which is what everyone wished you before you never heard from them again. The photograph is warm where you will not let it go. It circulates its black and white dream. Maybe it's your teenage daughter's face, caught inside you like a memory of yourself. You have tried to warn her without making her feel captive. You've tried to give her a counternarrative, revolutionary plot, but your imagination flints and dies each time you start telling a story. You shut up and go out to shovel snow like it's heaven-sent bullshit. When your daughter leaves the house, the punch line comes to you, and you shout it at her back: *do not turn around; do not turn into a tree, a statue, a stat, a cameo, a blazon, or a selfie. Do not turn into an image* is what no woman you know feels like telling her daughter. If this really is her portrait, no one would call what she is doing in the picture smiling. Even with her back turned, she looks unlikeable.

Gina

No woman I know watches her daughter get pulled away from her, like a wave receding after it crashes on the rocks.

No woman I know is a nude on that rock.

No woman I know is a monument carved into rock.

No woman I know coming out of the ocean endlessly rocking.

No woman I know gets to choose the person she wants to be: paper scissors rock rock rock rock.

No woman I know in the rain says, *look at the tears on that rock.*

No woman I know places a rock that she's been carrying in her fist on the gravestone.

No woman I know pelted a man when he was still a boy with a rock.

No woman I know says her mother was that rock.

No woman I know thinks this year has been a freakish rash of "Falling Rock."

No woman I know thinks the past has to be ancient to be made mute as rock.

No woman I know at the protest smiles and hands me a rock.

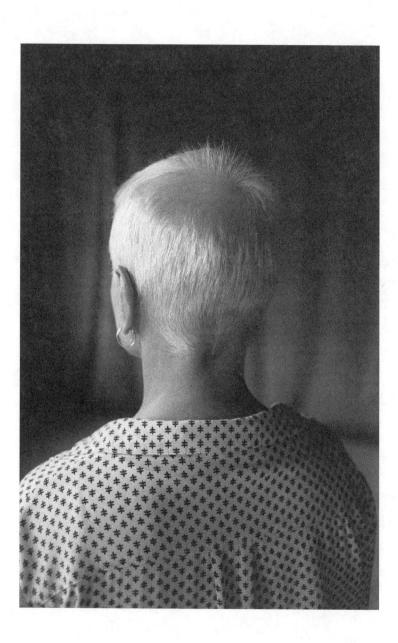

Lexi

No woman I know is your avatar.

No woman I know, with you looming behind her.

No woman I know is your guide, distraction, enemy, and muse.

No woman I know needs you to show her how to use the console.

No woman I know shows her daughter how to move around these streets undetected.

No woman I know keeps watch for the men—a glandular, unflagging anticipation.

No woman I know wants you to either see through her eyes or see through her.

No woman I know hates her body in this game.

No woman I know remembers what she was wearing.

No woman I know shows her daughter how to laugh and shrug it off.

No woman I know blasts bright holes in the night sky in order not to lose.

No woman I know hurls explosives at the dark hazards of men.

No woman I know hands one to her daughter and says, "watch this."

No woman I know throws her voice down the street, scattering the men.

No woman I know shows her daughter how to aim, dodge, and level up.

No woman I know wants to marry you in this game.

No woman I know hears your footsteps behind her.

No woman I know is unreal and gets a finite number of weapons for free.

No woman I know can shoot flames from her eyes.

No woman I know has lost her mouth to a hole in her head.

No woman I know with her empty speech bubbles floating away and popping.

No woman I know is all the women who turned around shouting.

No woman I know will turn into a statue of gold if you touch her.

No woman I know like a mirage at the end of the street.

No woman I know believes you were just a bad apple.

No woman I know urges her daughter to step into the reality where she feels she has no reality.

No woman I know shows her daughter how to change the street view.

No woman I know is trying to make it through the city before her character dies.

No woman I know understands that the men will see her coming.

No woman I know can get where she is going because of the golden apples the men keep rolling in her path.

No woman I know can tell the difference between the good and the bad ones.

No woman I know wants her daughter to believe that zero-sum worlds are the only ones possible.

No woman I know is a hole in her own daydream.

No woman I know lets her daughter loose in the game.

No woman I know sees her daughter running past the golden apples, not slowing or stooping, not looking down, not breaking her stride, not stopping.

Quinn

No woman I know will tell you jack if that woman is your mother.

No woman I know had language for it when it happened or knew how to stop it from feeling normal.

No woman I know is going to tell her daughter about the boy-friend who choked her or the one who kidnapped her briefly; the one who kept a gun hidden in their apartment. Not when she can't even get this daughter to take a nap and not later either.

No woman I know with earrings like hollowed eyes, earrings like looms unweaving her own body.

No woman I know says, no, you can't take her daughter's photograph.

No woman I know with the heavy shape of words that took years to form in her mouth.

No woman I know wears it around her eyes and draped across her shoulders like a dead body.

No woman I know was looking at something she wanted to show her daughter; she forgets what when she hears them say *give me a smile, slut, bitch, who do you think you are* like steps she won't follow to her building.

No woman I know zigzags through the city to lose the voices trapped inside her.

No woman I know caught in a maze of decoy eyes, shiny dream eyes, third-person eyes, photographed eyes that seem to watch her every move.

No woman I know is herself a blind spot with shiny earrings.

No woman I know, her eyes grow earrings like big dripping minutes.

No woman I know in a story she tells her daughter in order to interrupt the plot they find themselves in. "Look around," she says, "can you find your way out?"

No woman I know with fingers threading her daughter's fingers.

No woman I know wants to step into that light.

No woman I know is how I feel.

Shelly

No woman I know wants to help you today.

No woman I know wants to make eye contact and ask you questions.

No woman I know can unlisten to your troubles that are like no one else's.

No woman I know says she's sorry that happened to you.

No woman I know says "sorry" when you point out the stain on her shirt while dodging your hand trying to wipe it away.

No woman I know listens to your stories before anyone else arrives.

No woman I know says "sorry" when you ask to see her after work.

No woman I know learns a thousand ways of refusing without ever saying "no."

No woman I know teaches her daughter to say "no" and "yes" and "fuck you" and "I'm sorry."

No woman I know learned it from her mother, who said she was sorry more than she said any other thing, all day long.

No woman I know used to scream "stop apologizing" at her mother.

No woman I know with *sorrys* rising up and bursting inside of her.

No woman I know is sorry you don't recognize her outside of the office.

No woman I know said "sorry" when confronted with the bad checks she had written.

No woman I know is sorry you are groping her under the table while speaking to someone else.

No woman I know is sorry, but you can't catcall your grandchild when she walks into the room.

No woman I know is sorry you are yelling at her and beating the steering wheel with your fists and punching the rearview mirror.

No woman I know wants to be the kind of woman who says "sorry," or the kind of woman who accommodates and complains about it later to her friends.

No woman I know deletes the first sentence of her email that begins "I'm sorry," but the ghost of it remains, a shadow-word haunting all the other words.

No woman I know believes in ghosts or angels unless they are all named "sorry."

No woman I know can stop thinking "sorry" after snapping at her daughter.

No woman I know understands "sorry" as soft currency, a way to keep holding what's not there until it is there.

No woman I know with the nuanced social language of women on her lips.

No woman I know means what you think she means when she says she's sorry.

No woman I know means to plant the word inside you where it might ignite a feeling.

No woman I know feels the smoldering of all her *sorrys*.

No woman I know slows the *s*, where all the empathy accumulates.

No woman I know sounds like a fire when she says it.

No woman I know doesn't fantasize about arson.

No woman I know turned and ran from a burning living landscape.

No woman I know thinks burning is a way of saying sorry.

Hala

No woman I know trying on another woman's clothes.

No woman I know clears her throat and roots out a voice.

No woman I know shunts nervous circulations, currents of sweat and hormones.

No woman I know is the sound of her voice saying "yes, but."

No woman I know can breathe in this frame.

No woman I know says "escape artist" about herself.

No woman I know says "open book" about herself.

No woman I know is metaphoric, is allegorical, is symbolic, is cast for the wrong part.

No woman I know coincides with her own suspicions.

No woman I know as a girl practiced signing her name in other people's handwriting.

No woman I know wears a flower print and says "um" about her hair.

No woman I know on ketamine feels like a shadowy smudge in a painted tableau.

No woman I know on ketamine looks into her own crystal skull.

No woman I know panicked and casting around for a pronoun.

No woman I know with a hushing pronoun, hot in her mouth, trying to spit it out.

No woman I know answers "my silhouette" on the magazine quiz.

No woman I know answers "neither" to the question on a personality test, though that is not an option.

No woman I know with a sibilant tip of a pronoun slippery on her tongue, accusatory, demanding, exhilarating.

No woman I know coincides with her own tradition.

No woman I know made it possible to speak of herself.

Alex

No woman I know slips through the cracked door unnoticed.

No woman I know walks off her anger for as long as it takes.

No woman I know hurries into a future where there's only more winter in the middle of the country.

No woman I know walking away from a time she would not have escaped being burned, hanged, drowned, or locked away.

No woman I know because steps are procedures for forgetting.

No woman I know thinks *what will he do without me?*

No woman I know and a plague of mockingbirds.

No woman I know sets off along the soft roads where there's no longer a field behind the house or doors that won't lock.

No woman I know mapped her route beyond this vanishing point.

No woman I know and a plague of footprints.

No woman I know short-circuits among rabbit holes smelling like minerals and remembers scum rings in the tub, the kitchen sink, stacked high.

No woman I know recovers her footing and moves on.

No woman I know slips off the path and onto another and another, each leading to the same house.

No woman I know and a plague of amnesias.

No woman I know retreats into a very realistic flashback.

No woman I know looks for a story about herself to stride into and take with her like a souvenir.

No woman I know and a plague of dolls.

No woman I know walks backward into the portrait.

No woman I know has a face emerging from the back of her head.

No woman I know leaves the flashlight in her pocket.

No woman I know craves the blankness of water and follows a river.

No woman I know thinks there might be a horse for her up ahead.

No woman I know turns toward an insensate patch of sky thinking *better to be incomplete.*

No woman I know and a plague of holes.

No woman I know walks herself into the sweet everlasting blur.

No woman I know changes her mind and can walk around after she dies.

Marissa

No woman I know lives her life as if watching a black-and-white movie in which she is the protagonist.

No woman I know pins her location.

No woman I know calls to tell you where she is right now.

No woman I know overexposes her sky to show you a storm is coming.

No woman I know is the first one to hang up.

No woman I know escapes the frame, the corner, the courtyard, the speeding car, careening and skidding toward your imagination.

No woman I know realizes she is watching a blizzard roll into the movie when the landscape blanches and chokes, desperate to become a character.

No woman I know in the fog that will never burn off.

No woman I know looks down through layers of ice and sees shadows swimming under her skin.

No woman I know asks, *what can't you see?* Nothing in the picture goes untouched by whiteness, even when she knows not to believe in it.

No woman I know hasn't grown up inside this movie.

WHITE NOISE NOCTURNE
(Tour of Ypsilanti)

You cannot click through this darkness. Night is not a sleeping screen; it is not the back of god. It offers no image except your own memory, which is an imaginary film. Even though it's impossible to tell where the music is coming from and how much of it we carry inside us, we follow the imaginary film's soundtrack. Walking in the dark, we need something to follow. Walking in the dark is like trying to see our own whiteness, which is everywhere and therefore impossible to locate. We can't walk away from it, we must follow sketchy outlines, whiffs, and barely audible voices. Our soundtrack isn't cinematic because there's no climax, no convulsive, sudden pitch. It lingers and latches on, the collective cries of *no*, the ghostly acoustics of marvelous dogs and fallen machines, as we walk through this former sundown town. Our ears sensitize as the night falls. Soon, you'll start to hear it, a white tinnitus, a vague complaint whining in your skull.

Here's a nice marshy place to grapple with your own fictions. Built on a swamp, Ypsilanti can best be described as shifty. Long ago, workers buried streams in clay pipes under the water table and sunk tiles to absorb soggy earth. On this wetland, we've built a thousand buildings, acting like a thousand microphones that conduct the murmurings of the underworld. When you stand in a house built on top of unfathomable depth, you don't have to wonder why you hear things. Each building contains the memory of someone taken away or sent back, someone made to stay against their will, someone beaten or shot or raped. Inside buildings, viral viruses and rooting roots come into earshot. Pipes gurgle and gasp. Used to be that Black workers went home before the sun set, before the town went fully werewolf, before it tipped into vampiric violence. Digging the noises up from the ground, pulling the sounds down to the page. Either way, once you hear it, you must remember it doesn't belong to you. Even as you narrativize it or copwatch for the young man handcuffed with his face in the grass as the maskless cop spits at you and keeps saying that he has seen you before.

This is an example of something you could not hear before but now is loud and clear. The white rooms filling with white noise; the clouds of explanations, judgments, and corrections; whole zones of white volume impossible to turn down because someone broke the knob off, because it's ambient, always already there, already happening. Because we keep exhaling it and saying it doesn't exist. Saying, "What noise?" Saying, "I don't talk like that." Saying, "I don't see ghosts." Saying, "There you go again." Because the white judge cried when she convicted the white shooter. She said her hand was forced. Her voice cracked; "it's not about race," she said through white tears. Because you remember your own tears when the cop pulls you over again and again as a teenager, never once giving you a ticket. Each cop giving you a gentle or stern warning until you feel your own inner siren coming on each time you hear a state siren. It is you they blare for.

When a Black man comes to your porch asking for money, what do you do? Or a Black woman driving home late one night gets into an accident and steps into the porch light of your home to ask for help. What do you do? The porch is a soft threshold, a gravitational pull, a suspension of time. A porch raises but cannot settle questions of belonging. A person might be walking around lost in the dark, or on your porch, knocking on your door. You probably know that Detroit is the most segregated city in America. Within city limits, it's also the least diverse. White people live in a wraparound porch called the suburbs. Read: no solicitors, wet paint, guard dog. A porch cannot completely hide what is on the inside. Half an hour outside of Detroit, our neighborhood listserv instructs us: *Please lock your doors and keep your porch lights on. Call the police for even minor incidents.* A porch clings to its house.

You can't tell by looking, even in the daytime, but this was a stop on the Underground Railroad, where Elijah McCoy transported fugitive slaves in a false bottom of his wagon. He also patented "the real McCoy"—a lubricating cup for factory machines—and the lawn sprinkler, which helped domesticate and divvy up the prairie, making tidy lawns for nuclear families. Ypsilanti's white noise is like a sprinkler moving back and forth over the entire town. If you are in the stream, you feel the humming vibrate your cavities. You feel its pulse up through your feet. You think: *Are those people in the park being too loud? What is that man even doing here? Or that loitering car stereo too heavy on the 808s? Does something feel not quite right?* When I put it like that, you know exactly what these thoughts are lubricating.

Tracing the noise's origins is complicated by who hears it, and when and where. In 1914, workers made this road, Michigan Avenue, running ultimately between Chicago and Detroit. Before this, the route was the Great Sauk Trail. All the other streets are one-way, letting commuters get through fast. Residents, however, feel enmeshed in a kind of sonic plaid, something like a Celtic electric fence. We feel the vacuum effect of cars leaving town, radios jamming. The push-pull of opposing traffic directions creates a Doppler effect of sirens on Arcade Street. This street should be named David Ware Street, after the man the cops shot here, or Ware Street, a pun not lost on you. Where do we find ourselves? Staying and leaving, this is our signature sound. You have to know who you are to hear if the sirens are moving toward you or away.

We adopt filters for our ears, or we believe our filters dissolved when we heard the recording of our mayor's racist remarks, the mayor we voted for. We made a racket outside her house until she resigned. Then we believe we are hearing as if for the first time; virgin listening comes with the usual nausea and regret. We recall the landmarks: here is where I strung up a piñata for my white daughter's birthday party; here is where I wore box braids and extensions; here is where I told my students to "powwow" about a poem; here is where I had my reasons. I do not know if speaking of filters will help us become sensible to the meanings of filibustering, vocal thunder, choral outrage, a loud silent cringe, or the graduated spectrum of screams. Can you hear beyond the clamor of another white crisis? Here is where, in 1867, Frederick Douglass spoke about overconfidence and false hope in the White House; he spoke out against a president acting as if he were king, and his incendiary words caught in the wind. Words have nothing on the wind. Later a fire destroyed the entire third floor of this building.

What do you imagine hides in the dark? This is exactly the wrong question. Immediately we become nostalgic for a time when it was unquestionably the right question. You cannot step through that time neatly into another. You carry it with you like a virus, like the sound of starlight reaching you in another century. Remember half of what you hear is tinnitus, a sound your brain makes up to keep you from knowing you are alone. Tinnitus, linked etymologically to the jingling of coins, is like the sound of capitalism, a sound we've invented to keep us from ourselves. Whole cities suffer it. You keep working through the uprising, you keep working as if the world needs you. You stand by a bar and wait for it to open. You rent a house with good Wi-Fi by the lake for a couple weeks. You stand by the mailbox and wait for a new shipment to arrive. You cannot remember what you ordered, but your dog knows the engine pitch of the Amazon truck.

Imagine your native tongue being pulled out of your mouth. Imagine that in order to be heard, you must stuff your mouth with someone else's words, pronunciation, cadence, and vocal dynamics. Imagine that what you might say cannot be parsed. Words flatten and derange. Your vowels shred. Your echo snaps the syntax of your sentence, breaks your sense of belonging. Remember the panic of the girl running down the street crying, lost maybe, absolutely scared, and you cannot recall enough Spanish to help her? All your high grades will not help this girl find her peace or her family. Nonetheless, you correct your child when they come home from school speaking Black vernacular. Yes, it's the language of their friends; yes, it is a rich language; no, they cannot have it too. The white noise coming out of our own faces congeals in amnesia about who built these roads and logics. Ypsilanti's throat throbs with languages that are impossible to disentangle unless you ignore everything you don't understand.

Can we understand the acoustics of a place by referring to our own experiences of it, or is it best to go back further? We have come to the mostly demolished Ford bomber plant from World War II, designed by Albert Khan, once a mile-long assembly line that built half of all the B-24 Liberators. You can't hear the protests of all the white Rosie the Riveters who did not want to work with Black Rosies, but you wouldn't be wrong if you did. All their daughter's daughters, all of us, not meaning any harm yet going to the police, *please help me,* offloading our violence and complicity. On this spot is where that history gathered around the tidy visual propaganda of a white woman flexing.

Just look at our confused and embarrassed images reflected in the
storefront window. We can see our mouths moving but can't hear
what we are saying, even to ourselves. Can you hear through *what
are you doing here* to the *get the fuck out* it contains? We barely
even hear the false confessions dripping and welling up inside us.
We keep walking into white noise, like wind trapped in a con-
demned house, panicked, shrieking between cracks in the boarded-
up windows and slamming the doors over and over. See the window
reflected in the window? In this room, when a student explains to
the Judiciary Board why he was protesting racist vandalism on
campus, no one can hear what he's saying. When he tells them
what he hears at the sight of a white cop with a gun, the Board
shoots their incredulous *really?* and condescending *now there* into
his testimony. When he tells them the cop's voice wasn't what he
was listening to that night, all their heads cock, lips smirked. What
they hear is *yes* or *no,* but mostly *no.* What they hear is a vacuum in the room next door. What they can't hear is the ever-pres-
ent sound of fourteen to forty gunshots coming from behind, and
before that the sound of bulldozing a Native burial ground to make
a "Center." What we hear now accompanies the silencing of what
we once heard; everything we hear is echoed in full absence, full
eerie mourning.

I have forgotten to tell you about the river. It organizes the city's
sonic inventories. Right now, it sounds like an open digestive
track. Only so much can be broken down or absorbed. The banks
of the river are the best place to imagine your own death. You
remember the world you once lived in, and you had to kill that
life. It bothered you that the sun was always frozen or sweating in
the postcard you sent back; nostalgia divvied up time into when
we didn't believe in two worlds and when we couldn't escape
two worlds. We who are left have volunteered for the future, of
which we are already ashamed. Ypsilanti was once the intersection
of several trails formed by four tribes: the Wyandot, Chippewa,
Ottawa, and Potawatomi. Their early settlements along the Huron
River are where our city's story begins. We have shoved these stories into little pockets of deafness all around town. As you walk,
notice the vacant buildings; think about those buildings holding
absence, like museums of erasure, like holding cells for hidden
lives, like small monuments to missing or incarcerated people, like
hotel rooms waiting for the next economic wave.

What you can't see is that our city looks destroyed. If you can't feel it, put your finger in a bullet hole in the wall and scream. Abandonment stretches into something just alive enough to crawl under the porch and die. We who live here have an affection for deserted things as if umbilically attached to disappointment. If you suspect that everything you've heard on this tour is fraudulent, the piped-in soundtrack of the new cinema, I cannot say for sure that you are wrong. Sounds outside our hearing range tend to cause ominous feelings and colorful hallucinations. If you are getting the feeling that Ypsilanti is a cage designed to make you inaudible, know that your ears are the first paranoid organ. In this way the place resembles Caucasia, the fabled land between the breaking waves of the Black and Caspian Seas, where our narcissistic disorder began. On this very spot in 1958, three white men, each believing himself to be Jesus Christ, were put in the same room at the Ypsilanti State Hospital. There they remained until their loneliness made them friends, and they refused to destroy one another's identity. All three heard voices telling them who they were, but only the youngest of the Christs eventually tuned in to another frequency and morphed into someone more imaginative. Can you pluck a single voice out of the pitchy tangle of crisscrossing signals? Do you know which one is yours? Do you find your own thoughts become louder when a white man is talking?

ACKNOWLEDGMENTS

Grateful acknowledgment to the women—Farnoosh Fathi, Trish Flanigan, Georgia Herold, Margaret Takako Hicken, Melissa Jones, Anna Maria Hong, Susan McCarty, Christina Milletti, Linette Lao, Laura Larson, Claudia Rankine, and Deb Olin Unferth—whose conversations about and alongside this book have helped shape it and whose friendships I hold dear. Thanks to Eastern Michigan University for their generous support and especially to my students for their commitments to justice and language, in and outside of class. Thanks to everyone who played tennis with me since summer 2020, especially Wendy Langrock, for bringing your fierce joy and focus. All my love to Jeff Clark for being there every step of the way.

Juna Hume Clark made writing this book possible/necessary and informed all the best parts of it. This book is for her.

Many thanks to the editors of these journals who published early versions or excerpts of the essays here: *Boston Review, Columbia Journal, CRAFT, Ninth Letter, Notre Dame Review, PANK, Journal of Narrative Theory, The Rupture, Slag Glass City,* and *The Spectacle.* Thanks especially to Catherine Taylor and Nicholas Muellner of Image Text Ithaca Press who published *Question Like a Face* as a gorgeous, limited-edition chapbook, with images by Jeff Clark.

Rest in Power Aura Rosser and women everywhere killed by state and domestic violence.

Portraits by Laura Larson with much gratitude for her subjects' palpable and plural fortitudes, in order of appearance:

Mariana, 2019
Dani, 2018
Sandra, 2020
Lucille, 2019
Natascia, 2020
Dionne, 2020
Hala, 2020
Lexi, 2019
Quinn, 2018
Gina, 2019
Shelly, 2018
Alex, 2019
Marissa, 2019

SELECTED SOURCES

Conversations with abolitionists and activists, as well as an abundance of journalism, police reports, legal documents, and academic papers, throughout writing this book have been invaluable. Here is a very partial list of texts that informed my thinking and writing.

Anonymous. *People's Retort to the Prosecutor's Report.* Radical Washtenaw, April 2, 2015.

Barthes, Roland. *Mythologies.* Translated by Annette Lavers, Farrar, Straus & Giroux-Noonday, 1972.

Brooks, Gwendolyn. *Riot.* Broadside, 1969.

Cacho, Lisa Marie. *Social Death: Racialized Rightlessness and the Criminalization of the Unprotected.* New York UP, 2012.

Cixous, Hélèn. "Fiction and Its Phantoms: A Reading of Freud's *Das Unheimlich* (The 'Uncanny')." *Volleys of Humanity: Essays 1972–2009.* Edited by Eric Prenowitz, Edinburgh UP, 2011.

DuPont Textile Fibers Product Information. Audiovisual Collections and Digital Initiatives Department, Hagley Museum and Library.

Ernaux, Annie. *The Years.* Translated by Alison Strayer, Seven Stories Press, 2017.

Federici, Silvia. *Witches, Witch-Hunting, and Women.* PM Press, 2018.

Hamad, Ruby. *White Tears/Brown Scars: How White Feminism Betrays Women of Color.* Catapult, 2020.

Handley, Susannah. *Nylon: The Story of a Fashion Revolution.* Johns Hopkins UP, 1999.

Hartman, Saidiya. *Wayward Lives, Beautiful Experiments: Intimate Histories of Social Upheaval.* Norton, 2019.

Hermes, Matthew. *Enough for One Lifetime: Wallace Carothers, Inventor of Nylon.* Chemical Heritage Foundation, 1996.

Irigaray, Luce. *Marine Love of Friedrick Nietzsche.* Translated by Gillian C. Gill, Columbia UP, 1991.

Lorde, Audre. *Zami: A New Spelling of My Name.* Crossing Press, 1982.

Miller, Chanel. *Know My Name.* Penguin, 2020.

Morrison, Toni. *Playing in the Dark: Whiteness and the Literary Imagination.* Harvard UP, 1992.

Rose, Jacqueline. *On Violence and On Violence Against Women.* Farrar, Straus & Giroux, 2021.

Rukeyser, Muriel. *The Collected Poems of Muriel Rukeyser.* Edited by Janet E. Kaufman and Anne F. Herzog, U of Pittsburgh P, 2005.

Smith, Seba. "A Corpse Going to a Ball." *The Rover* (Maine), 28 Dec., 1843.

Srinivasan, Amina. *The Right to Sex: Feminism in the Twenty-First Century.* Farrar, Straus & Giroux, 2021.

Thompson, A. K. "Did Someone Say Riot?" *Premonitions: Selected Essays on the Culture of Revolt.* AK Press, 2018.

Vuong, Ocean. *On Earth We're Briefly Gorgeous.* Penguin, 2019.

Wang, Jackie. *Carceral Capitalism.* Semiptext(e), 2018.

White, Rachel Rabbit. *Porn Carnival.* Wonder, 2019.

Wypljewski, Joann. *What We Don't Talk About When We Talk About #MeToo: Essays on Sex, Authority, and the Mess of Life.* Verso, 2020.

Zilg, Gerard Colby. *Du Pont: Behind the Nylon Curtain.* Prentice-Hall Englewood, 1974.

21ST CENTURY ESSAYS
David Lazar and Patrick Madden, Series Editors

This series from Mad Creek Books is a vehicle to discover, publish, and promote some of the most daring, ingenious, and artistic nonfiction. This is the first and only major series that announces its focus on the essay—a genre whose plasticity, timelessness, popularity, and centrality to nonfiction writing make it especially important in the field of nonfiction literature. In addition to publishing the most interesting and innovative books of essays by American writers, the series publishes extraordinary international essayists and reprint works by neglected or forgotten essayists, voices that deserve to be heard, revived, and reprised. The series is a major addition to the possibilities of contemporary literary nonfiction, focusing on that central, frequently chimerical, and invariably supple form: The Essay.

Everything I Never Wanted to Know
CHRISTINE HUME

Engine Running: Essays
CADE MASON

Ripe: Essays
NEGESTI KAUDO

Dark Tourist: Essays*
HASANTHIKA SIRISENA

Supremely Tiny Acts: A Memoir of a Day
SONYA HUBER

Art for the Ladylike: An Autobiography through Other Lives
WHITNEY OTTO

The Terrible Unlikelihood of Our Being Here
SUSANNE PAOLA ANTONETTA

Warhol's Mother's Pantry: Art, America, and the Mom in Pop*
M. I. DEVINE

How to Make a Slave and Other Essays
JERALD WALKER

---

*Annual Gournay Prize Winner